KING DONALD KHRUMP

A Khrump to Trump and Dump Them All

PHIL O. REILLY

KKingdom Books

King Donald Khrump
A Khrump to Trump and Dump Them All
All Rights Reserved.
Copyright © 2018 Phil O. Reilly
v4.0

This is a work of fiction. The events and characters described herein are imaginary and are not intended to refer to specific places or living persons. The opinions expressed in this manuscript are solely the opinions of the author and do not represent the opinions or thoughts of the publisher. The author has represented and warranted full ownership and/or legal right to publish all the materials in this book.

This book may not be reproduced, transmitted, or stored in whole or in part by any means, including graphic, electronic, or mechanical without the express written consent of the publisher except in the case of brief quotations embodied in critical articles and reviews.

KKingdom Books

ISBN: 978-0-578-20047-7

Library of Congress Control Number: 2018930403

Cover Photo © 2018 thinkstockphotos.com. All rights reserved - used with permission.

PRINTED IN THE UNITED STATES OF AMERICA

My name is Phil O. Reilly. My career with Fix News is well known throughout the news media landscape and has been followed by many, from my colleagues in the industry and those in broadcasting school hoping to break into the entertainment news field, all the way down to my adorably undereducated yet beloved Fix News fans. Being a well-seasoned news entertainment professional with a wide spectrum of talents, I even helped to create our unofficial in-house Fix slogan, "It ain't news 'til we Fix it!" While I admit I've been controversial at times, I've always accepted it as the honorable cost of doing business in the political entertainment news world. It takes guts and sacrifice, and it's certainly not for everyone.

For a little while now, since King Donald's coronation, I've been besieged by my network, my many fans, and the great King Donald Khrump's fan base representatives to write an official historical and biographical account of the great Donald's first one hundred days as king as they unfold. I accepted the challenge not simply for the large bonus and royalties contract, but more because I consider it an honor to write what I am absolutely sure will become "The Official Fix News Network's Kingdom of the Northern Noble Lands Standard Informational Resource for All Things Related to the Great King Donald Khrump and the First One Hundred Days of His Incredible Reign."

For my entire career, I've respected and adored my viewers and fans, and I promise to put the same uncompromising accuracy and integrity into this book as I've always put into my reporting as well as into my Fix Network show *The No-Turn Zone*. I consider the act of writing this book to be a "giving back" to the "little people" who have faithfully enjoyed my special kind of excellence over my entire incredible career.

As we all know, the amazing King Donald Khrump resides in the highest office of our land. His coronation ceremony was just over one month ago, and yet, that one month, so filled with intensity and outright fun, has felt like a year. I have a feeling, as so many do, that by the time he completes his first one hundred days, they will have been the most spectacular and amazingly creative first one hundred days ever by a king in the history of our kingdom. Every day when I wake up and check my Fix News Network feed, I always see something new that he's done that is far, far beyond anything I or anyone else ever could have expected.

My plan for this book is to first spend a few short pages on his early development as a newborn human-ape hybrid, followed by a somewhat detailed history of his important formative years. A short synopsis of the debates leading up to the election will come next, followed by a personal journal style recounting of his first one hundred days, where I'll focus principally on the highlights as they occur as his vision for our kingdom's future changes from an idea to a reality. My own personal journal that I'll continue to write will be my guide.

What an amazing future our kingdom has in store. The possibilities are wide open, and I'm sure with King Donald's guidance, it will be better than we ever imagined, or, as King Donald likes to say, "Our kingdom will be greater and more amazingly amazing than ever before!"

Chapter One

His Early Years

Donald, as we all know, is special. After all, being the world's first human-gorilla hybrid is no small deal. Our future King Donald was born in Experimental Ward C of the New Days RNC/FIX Charity Hospital, a superbly modern experimental hospital built by funds donated by both the Repugnican National Committee and the Fix News Network. Shortly after being removed from his plastic cryovac-like birthing pouch, Donald, at the time known only as RNCFIX-00001X, was hosed down, sprayed with a cool gel, wrapped in foil, and then whisked down the hall on a pushcart to the cubicle that contained Pella, his personal genetically modified, nutritionally specific, superbly enhanced one nipple milking sow. Once there, he was lifted from the cart and gently placed at Pella's side, where he remained for most of the first year of his life.

My reader may be asking himself, 'Why was there even a hybrid project in the first place?" The answer? Inspiration. Inspiration from the "Man Upstairs." It began when The

Repugnican National Committee, in the middle of an influence drought, feeling wholly frustrated with its inability to influence social and governmental institutions, decided it was time to change its brand. For years, the terribly naive Dreamocratic National Committee had been blindly yet effectively pushing its irresponsible and cancerous so-called "fairness and equality" policies through both our government and our social networks. Yes, they may have meant well, but that certainly did not make it right. Such government enforced "fairness" completely ignored the important value of class competitiveness, which the "human animal" needs. The poor confused leaders of the DNC seemed to spend every waking moment of their lives looking for ways to try to take the "animal" out of the "human animal." They desperately needed to be stopped.

The RNC leaders knew the only way to stop them and take back control would be by changing the average citizen's perception of the RNC brand. There needed to be an RNC identity revolution, so to speak. The brand had to be made bolder and more exciting than ever before--and yet, how? The RNC leaders pooled their minds, and after much deliberation, decided to bring in the controversial celebrity figure D.P. Pruddit to be both their lead visionary and policy decision maker. Pruddit, an accomplished bioengineer and the former CEO and creative force behind the Love Your Pet More Toy Co., the sometimes controversial pet love-toy manufacturer, had long been considered a maverick in the fields of abstract genetics and social deconstruction. The RNC leaders, impressed with his unique résumé, realized he would be a perfect fit for their social sensibilities.

Pruddit and I, by the way, have been friends for many years and I've always seen him as a unique and exciting individual. I've also purchased and enjoyed using many of his company's love-toys with my purebred pet mastiffs Adolf and Helmut. You can believe me when I tell you that if you'd like to have a better relationship with your pets, his amazing and unique products are well worth the price and will take your relationship to a new and deeper level.

Pruddit brilliantly decided the first step on the road to finding inspiration for the RNC's new identity would be for him and the RNC leaders to isolate themselves at the exclusive spa Nirvana Lives Here, where they would search for holy guidance and inspiration. For many months the group prayed, meditated, and participated in the daily special Nirvana Lives Here holistic group penetrating massage. It was exhausting work, but finally, after many months, they had a breakthrough. Pruddit himself received a vision from the "Man Upstairs." He told me about his experience during an interview on my show a few years ago. He told me it came to him during a particularly strenuous deep-tissue penetrating massage session.

"With my eyes tightly shut, and with all my concentration on the tingling sensation of the massage oil, I suddenly saw God right there on the insides of my eyelids! It was a dark but very clear image of God! The image faded in a moment and was replaced by a gentle light. A moment later, the image of God returned, this time brighter. It stayed a few moments longer, but then faded again. I was feeling confused and didn't know what to think about the whole thing, but then right at that moment a brilliant light appeared to me which then transformed into a brilliant, shining image of God! As you can imagine, I was completely stunned by the whole experience! It had such a wonderful and obviously deep meaning for myself as well as the RNC! The message was so clear! God and light! God light! It was brilliant, totally brilliant!"

I asked him to explain further.

"Phil, it was absolutely crystal clear to me what it meant. You see, there's light beer and there's light-calorie snack chips, so why not light God? See how simple that is? The new RNC would make God light a part of their policy platform! They would use God as a kind of flavoring to be sprinkled on the policies of the new RNC. A little God here, a little God there, a little God everywhere! To keep everyone on the same page I even made sure that everyone involved in RNC policy decisions would have a symbolic can labeled "God Sprinkles" to remind them of what we were doing. Keep in mind, there was no traditional kind of God stuff, just a light sort of prop idea with small mentions of God everywhere.

"You see, Phil, the God Light policies of the RNC would appeal to the great masses of simple people, lazy thinkers, and, in particular, the undereducated. All those rocket scientists and PhD's and smarty-pants critical thinkers would of course stay with the Dreamocrats, but that was okay because there were so few of them anyway. There were plenty of ignorant kingdom citizens available to become the new RNC's backbone. God Light completely captured the imagination of the underclasses."

I then asked him how his bioengineering background influenced his decisions while transforming the RNC.

"Well, Phil, I felt it was an incredibly brilliant move by the 'Man Upstairs' to choose me in particular to receive his vision. With my bioengineering background, it was very easy for me to come up with a course of action on how to reverse the damaging effects the Dreamocrats' policies had made to our kingdom, specifically, the removal of respect for our animal instincts from government and social institution policies. I knew we needed to do something big, really big, to bring back the respect. Feeling inspired, I decided to pursue an idea of mine that I had dreamed of for so many years, but had never had the funding to pursue. It was a project I named 'Make Men More,' a human/ animal hybrid splicing program. After a series of divinely influenced coin tosses, we decided the first hybrid blend would be human/gorilla. With that decided, we began." That, reader, is when our future king's story began as well.

From the first moment young Donald was placed with Pella, the RNC leaders and lab researchers all felt that Pruddit's plan for a future of bold and exciting RNC styled science was well on its way. Young Donald loved cuddling with Pella, and she seemed to completely enjoy being a temporary mother to the young baby hybrid. For many months, they were inseparable, and everything was going perfectly well. However, that changed one day when something completely unexpected happened. You see, young Donald, a voracious eater, had been sucking endlessly on Pella's one poor teat, and, after nearly a year, with her body trying so hard to keep up with Donald's nutritional needs, there was nearly nothing left of her. Poor Pella was exhausted, drained, and frustrated.

Young Donald, frustrated as well by the single shriveling teat, displayed again for the umpteenth time the insane bratty temper that he is now so famous for. This time, however, was different. Poor Pella! When Donald finally calmed down after the attack, there were only small scattered pieces left of her. Donald had ripped her apart with the razor-sharp nails on his small but strong infant hands. Now, this was a huge setback for the experiment because Pella was one of only two pigs who had been genetically engineered to produce the proper nutrition for Donald's unique physiology. The researchers were not certain if Donald's early physiological development was complete, so to be sure, they sent word for the replacement pig to be sent to the hospital immediately. Unfortunately, they were informed that the second pig had been sold to a wealthy businessman friend of the chief hospital administrator to help raise money for the ward. The wealthy businessman, in the process of expanding his unique family zoo, was not about to let go a unique specimen that no one else in the world had.

This was of course the man who was to become Donald's adoptive father, the great Fritz Khrump. Fritz was a multi-millionaire real estate developer and entrepreneur, with a taste for the unusual, to say the least. The Khrump family zoo had been developed over many decades and had truly unique examples of animal life from all over the world. Fritz, being a champion negotiator, was not about to turn over this unique pig to the ward unless there was something better to be gained from the trade.

Now, to be honest, at that time, some of the researchers had had misgivings about Donald and his temper, and even questioned the wisdom of continuing with the experiment. Gorillas, being gentle and loving creatures, were typically not known to be violent and unpredictable, and yet that was the behavior Donald had displayed over and over and over again. Some of the members of the science staff even thought Donald should have been destroyed, after which the ward would have started fresh with a new subject made using a different and better splicing technique. Lucky for Donald, however, one of the lead lab technicians reminded everyone that destroying Donald was never an option because of how the hand of the "Man Upstairs" had been the guiding force behind the experiment in the first place. Plus, I was told he pointed out, even if they were to do the unthinkable, they would still need the Pella clone for the next hybrid, and they didn't have her.

After much deliberation and discussion, the head of the research lab called Mr. Fritz with a fantastic proposal. The lab offered Donald, an obviously unique zoo specimen, as a trade in exchange for the Pella clone. The researchers had decided that Donald would probably do well as an exotic pet as long as he was provided a simple diet of fresh fruit and vegetables. Satisfied that Donald would be well cared for, the researchers felt they could begin anew with a replacement hybrid specimen. Little did they know, however, their first and best-ever specimen would be going out the door. Donald's adventure into the world would begin. When offered the deal, Fritz, being a shrewd businessman and master negotiator, felt as if the most incredible deal of his life was being handed to him on a twenty-four-karat solid-gold Tiffany platter, so he jumped at the chance. Best....Deal....Ever! Amazing!

Chapter Two

Fritz Khrump had plans for Donald. Big plans. Would Donald be the star attraction of the Khrump family zoo that he would show off to his family and wealthy friends? Hardly. Fritz saw something so much bigger in Donald. Fritz saw himself. He saw what he himself could have been if he had had better genes, but Donald? What potential! After just a few months, Fritz realized how many opportunities would be available for Donald because of his super strength, dominating personality, and powerfully gorgeous executive hair. With training, Fritz knew Donald would develop not only his ability to control himself, but also the ability to control others around him. Remember, though, at the time, Donald was still only a zoo animal, a possession. Fritz would change that. He decided he would make Donald, this young hairy hybrid, his son. The son he always wanted but never had.

Fritz reasoned that with Donald having a 51%-49% human-ape gene ratio, he could receive full human rights and privileges after only a few short years of court battles. A true master negotiator, Fritz Khrump would make it happen, regardless of the sacrifices of time and money. Donald, such an obviously gifted and unique specimen, would be officially recognized by the world as a legitimate member of human society. Fritz was so sure of this, in fact, that even before Donald was officially recognized and given human status, his social skills training was well underway. It was very intense, but Fritz knew Donald could take it. The first step was being sure that Donald understood who was in charge. He had to understand that Fritz was in control and was his absolute master. Fritz's heavy hand made sure Donald learned that first lesson quickly.

Fritz Khrump loved being in control. His middle name was "Control." No, not really, but he wished it was. He loved controlling all things related to his family's affairs, and yet he wanted more—much, much more. Of course, Fritz had control over some aspects of regulations related to his business ventures because of his political donations, as all wealthy men had, and yes, he certainly found having that influence to be exciting, yet Fritz, never satisfied, still felt a deeper yearning, a yearning for influence on an extreme scale, a kingdom-wide scale. Now, owning Donald, he realized he could.

During the initial phases of his training, Donald, when upset, being such a playful spirit, would throw rocks. Sometimes, he'd throw garbage. Sometimes he'd even throw shit--his own, or anyone else's for that matter. Donald really liked to throw shit. Fritz, quickly identifying Donald's fun-loving temperament, decided he would teach him his own methods on how to throw shit in the most effective way.

The issue of Donald's temper had been spoken of briefly during the trade, and at the time, it almost seemed as if it might have been a defect of some sort. Fritz, however, wisely realized that Donald's bratty temper could actually be a key to Donald's amazing future, given the proper guidance. Fritz decided he would teach Donald how his temper, properly directed, could be an incredible and effective tool.

Sometimes, I get on my knees and thank the "Man Upstairs" for having blessed the Khrump family with Donald. Although some may think of him as an idiot half-breed hairball knuckle-dragging primate with only the barest understanding of human culture and language, we, the members of the Repugnican National Committee, know him as our genius leader. I can only imagine what could have become of Donald in the hands of a Dreamocratic family. Those simpletons would most likely have taken him for psychiatric counseling or some other such nonsense instead of seeing his insane temper and shit throwing talents for what they really were; gifts from the "Man Upstairs."

Those gifts did, of course, need fine-tuning, but Fritz Khrump was prepared. He still had all the tools in hand that were left over from the raising of his daughters. All the tools that the typical rich family had. All the carrots and all the sticks. Fritz found out quickly though that corporal punishment and humiliation would only go so far when dealing with the likes of his new son. Donald, such a stubborn-minded individual and a firm believer in his obvious greatness, began showing resistance to some of the finer tuning his adopted father was trying to instill in him. While every Repugnican member now absolutely loves all things Donald, his father, at the time, had yet to understand how his son's raw intimidation and extreme vicious selfishness were to become some of Donald's most effective tools in his personal toolbox.

Fritz continued Donald's training for years, and the results were amazing. Unfortunately, even the most brilliantly laid plans can sometimes run into unexpected snags. Fritz

Khrump's friends, as supportive as they were in the beginning, began to resent how Donald developed so much quicker than their own children, and, feeling that Fritz was exposing them as incompetent parents, began turning into jealous enemies.

How do jealous enemies destroy dreams? They do it by lying. Rich, jealous enemies do it by lying on a grand scale with huge conspiracy-level lies. It started with lies about how Donald was being "too friendly" with some of their daughters. Obviously, there was a misunderstanding on the daughters' part concerning Donald's powerful physical charm. The parents, however, looking for ways to hurt the Khrump family name, saw the misunderstanding as an opportunity, and for a while they irresponsibly encouraged their daughters to stick to their stories.

Fritz, always a brilliant negotiator, arranged to meet secretly with the young girls without their parents' knowledge. During the meetings he passionately explained to the children about how the "Man Upstairs" would sometimes use just and proper men such as himself to punish liars, and, thankfully, the accusations were soon forgotten. I'm sure my readers understand as well as I do how young girls are prone to misunderstandings because of their vivid imaginations. Some even purposely make things up. All part of being a teenage girl, I suppose.

Unfortunately for Fritz and Donald, that was not to be the last of the accusations. Before they knew it, even more groups of unraveled, sick, and jealous parents had come forward with their daughters to make fresh insults to the Khrump family name. Oh, the terrible sin of jealousy! It can make even the most rational human being into a mass of vengeful emotional confusion! This time, however, the accusations were not just about touching, they were about actual assault! It was such an embarrassment for the Khrump family that even now, as I write this chapter in the life of our great King, I feel a deep, terrible sadness for the unfair pain our poor Donald had to endure, and at such an early age! Fritz Khrump, somehow managing to keep a calm disposition even in the face of such terrible lies, wisely chose the best course of action. Donald would continue his training abroad.

Chapter Three

The Halls of Kingdom Justice Military School in the city of Vladd was the best school in the Kingdom of Pruska, and it was no less than what Donald, our future King, deserved. King Andre Putenski, a longtime friend of Fritz Khrump, was only too happy to accept the young and charismatic Donald as a guest student at the exclusive school. Donald looked magnificent in his school uniform, and anyone who has ever seen photos of him from that time in his life would of course agree. His massive swath of thick golden hair literally burst out from under his school uniform cap. Such amazingly gorgeous hair!

Our beloved future king underwent an important image change at that point in his life. He and I, being such good friends for so many years now, will sometimes talk about that time. When I tease him about the dramatic changes to his appearance, our gracious king, always a sport, just smiles and says, "I think I cleaned up unbelievably well."

That was the time of his first full-body shave and the start of his electrolysis treatments. Gone was his oily, musky black fur: shuttled in was his now famous buttery turmeric tan. Why such a magnificent change? Simple. A special driving need to be different. Donald worked endlessly to develop a secret blend of powerful food dyes which he then combined with a secret salt scrub process he learned from King Andre. I wish I could say more but, even though we've been friends for so many years, he still won't fill me in on all the details.

Donald and King Andre, or "Pootypoo" as Donald came to call him, became fast friends from the moment Donald had enrolled at the school. King Andre, fascinated with Donald, and thrilled at the prospect of being able to study him close up, promised Donald that his experiences at the school would be not only enriching, but also intensely exciting and highly memorable. Wow, were they ever! Perfect grades! Amazing athleticism! Numerous awards for both! Even more amazing is how quickly all this was accomplished! Donald, being such an amazing student and athlete, quickly won both the admiration and the respect of all faculty and students alike! Our future king simply oozed excellence everywhere!

Tragically, Donald was to leave the school after only six months. Both he and the faculty felt it was intimidating to the other students to have to compete with someone with such incredible physical and mental gifts. Simply put, he had learned all they could possibly teach him, and there was nothing left for the school to do. The entire school teaching and administrative staff felt that if Donald stayed, the school would be guilty of keeping him from achieving his potential.

The letters of recommendation sent from his instructors to the headmaster were simply glowing with praise for the future king. Here are just a few excerpts.

"He needs to leave. There is nothing for him here. We

can't do any more for him," and "He intimidates the other students. Donald shouldn't be here."

Even Donald's physical education coach, after witnessing Donald's incredible act of balancing an entire month's worth of his own feces in a perfect column behind a storage shed near the athletic field wrote of Donald, "I had no idea you could stack shit that high."

Loving, unselfish, and adoring words from such conscientious and caring faculty members. What else is there to say? Only that they loved him, but had to let him go.

Chapter Four

After leaving the school, Donald was invited by King Andre to spend some time with the Putenski Family Carnival Circus. Like the Khrump Family Zoo, the circus prided itself on having some of the most exotic and unique animal specimens from around the world, although it's mainstay of pride came from its world-class professional circus acts. The Putenski Circus was created with the express purpose of being entertainment for the immediate members of the Putenski family only, although on occasion, on certain official Pruskan Kingdom holidays, the Putenski family would graciously allow for discount performances to be available for the public.

King Andre was aware of how much Donald loved his own family zoo, so he thought Donald would appreciate spending some time there. King Andre was so very right. It was another wonderful experience for our future King Donald! During that time, King Andre and Donald became such good friends that together they would sometimes play pranks on the circus performers and management staff. An ongoing favorite joke of theirs was to have King Andre go for his early morning walk while holding a leash connected to Donald, who was wearing a collar! So funny! They would pretend to have training classes in the center ring in one of the big tops every day! They were some serious pranksters! Some of the performers who were not in on the joke would sometimes ask questions like, "Why spend so much time with that half-breed gorilla? There are others here too, and that one's going back soon."

King Andre, continuing the joke, would say something like "Oh, don't worry about that. I will teach this one to do tricks that you simply will not believe. He is well worth the time I'm putting in."

King Andre and Donald were unstoppable pranksters. Together, they had many, many seriously memorable good times.

One day, after many months of what must have felt like a nonstop holiday, Donald decided it was time to give something back to his hosts. Wanting to show his deep appreciation for all they had given him, he asked for and was given the job of painting special promotional signs for the upcoming holiday circus performances.

That symbolic show of appreciation is what led to the next step in Donald's spiritual growth. Painting the signs was a simple job, and yet Donald accomplished the work with such a fantastic artistic quality--so fantastic, in fact, that everyone in the kingdom simply could not stop talking about it. Everything Donald touched seemed to turn to gold.

Well, it wasn't very long until word of Donald's incredible reputation made its way to the very close and longtime friend of King Andre, the great King Arnold Shifenbakker of the kingdom of Austrinia. As I'm sure my readers remember, King Arnold Shifenbakker was the famous former circus strongman for the legendary Austrinian Circus. While King

Arnold had heard of Donald's many accomplishments at the Pruskan Halls of Kingdom Justice Military School, as well as his later artistic triumphs, King Arnold's main reason for wanting to meet Donald had more to do with Donald's unique interspecies physiology. Having maintained a lifelong interest in the physical sciences, he was hoping to study Donald close up, and perhaps find something valuable he could pass on to his own kingdom's citizens. King Shifenbakker always had the best interests of his kingdom's citizens in mind. Such a wise and loving king, although I'm sure everyone remembers stories of his time as a precocious youth when he had a reputation of being a somewhat loudmouth barbarian. I certainly do. It's hard to believe that such a reckless youth with such a cold, robotic personality could have matured into one of the most charismatic leaders alive today, and yet he did. King Arnold, feeling he just had to meet with Donald Khrump, sent a formal invitation to Donald inviting him to come for a two month stay at the Austrinian Royal Palace.

So began the two-month-long bromance between King Arnold and our Donald. By day they would fly fish in the kingdom's impeccably clean rivers and brooks, and by night they would enjoy a picnic by the grassy green edge where they would share bottle after bottle of great wines and spirits while eagerly learning more and more about each other. Throughout the night, their in-depth conversations covered all manner of subjects. Then came the wrestling. I suppose when two amazingly strong alpha males come together, it's bound to happen, and it did indeed happen. The security staff would allow the two of them about ten minutes of fun, and then they would break them up, clean them up, bandage wounds, sanitize the deeper bite marks, and set the bone breaks. Thankfully they both healed quickly and well, but there were times when members of the security staff had their concerns about what would happen and who would be blamed if the nightly fights were to go too far.

The weeks came and went very quickly. At the start of the eighth and last week of his visit, King Arnold and Donald were enjoying a wonderful afternoon poolside barbeque while discussing a possible extension to Donald's stay in the kingdom. After all, Donald had still not seen the beautiful fabled rocky western coastline, and it seemed a shame for him to leave before spending at least a few days there. Fate, however, was to intervene. This was the afternoon that Donald received an emergency call from home. Tragedy had struck. Poor Donald, frightened and confused, returned home immediately.

Fritz Khrump, his beloved father, did not have long to live. Fritz had been playing with the newest members of his zoo, an endangered snow leopard breeding pair that had just given birth to two cubs. Acquired from Nepal, Fritz wanted only the best for them, so he built a four-acre custom winter wonderland miniature mountainside enclosure for them. It was perfect in every way, and even had a one-way viewing mirror for the Khrump family and their guests to be able to view the snow leopards without having a negative influence on the animals' behavior.

Well, it turned out that the viewing mirror, quite adequate for most people, just wasn't enough for Fritz. Fritz decided that he wanted the snow leopards to be more like traditional pets. After all, he had paid quite a bit for the animals, and he was providing a perfect artificial environment for the entire family, so of course he felt, as any rational person would, that he was entitled to this one small pleasure. Now, I suppose some radical-minded extremist Dreamocrats might say that because the animals were on an endangered species list, he was not supposed to own them. Technically, because the animals had been taken from their wild home environment, perhaps they had been "stolen," or "traded illegally," but seriously, those terms completely ignore the fact that Fritz was putting in quite an effort to protect the species. All he wanted was one small family for personal pets! He had certainly worked long enough and hard enough to deserve at least that.

Unfortunately for Fritz, after entering the enclosure to make his claim, the ungrateful parents and cubs did not agree, and poor Fritz was scratched and bitten severely. Also, unfortunately for Fritz, the enclosure door had automatically locked after he had entered, and he had forgotten to bring his key. A few hours later he was found, alive, but sadly his cuts had become badly infected, and the infection had spread quickly. A message was sent immediately to Donald that he needed to get home as quickly as possible.

The largest master bedroom on the Khrump estate was transformed into an emergency intensive care unit. No expense had been spared. Some of the most talented specialists in the world had been flown in to monitor and care for Fritz's deteriorating condition. Fortunately, Donald arrived home and was able to spend a few hours at his father's bedside before he passed away. Fritz was eighty-six years old. Donald, being such a loving son, was completely devastated. Donald, however, was also mentally tough and had the ability to stay focused, and because of that he was able to begin "taking care of business" immediately. There were many responsibilities to be dealt with, both professional and personal, and Donald was eager to begin.

First up was deciding what was to be done with the snow

leopard family. Both parents and both cubs, were, of course, immediately destroyed. Yes, they were very beautiful and very rare, and yes, they were also quite endangered. However, as I and any other fantastic and powerful and successful and intelligent individual can understand, they did attack their owner-master. Such terrible behavior needed to be met with appropriate punishment, regardless of their unique, nearly extinct status. Donald was only too happy to take the responsible necessary action immediately. When done, Donald then tackled the most important professional economic responsibility: the reading of the will. He was again only too happy to immediately dispose of that necessity as well.

Fritz Khrump was both a classic learned philosopher and a wise modern businessman. He had the wisdom to know how Donald, being his son, though only a half-human hybrid, was still obviously far superior to his natural-born daughters. Thus, Fritz put complete control of the entire estate and finances into Donald's capable hands.

He knew that Donald would become the needed responsible patriarch of the family once he was gone, and as such he would take excellent care of and see to the needs of his sisters. Donald's sisters protested, of course. Females sometimes can become so excitable when faced with natural truths. What females fail to understand sometimes is that males graciously accept the heavily weighted responsibilities of taking care of females in order to protect them. It's just part of the male nature. His sisters did attempt to sue, but thankfully were rebuked by the just courts. After all, Fritz was of sound mind and body when his will was written, and because of that, there was nothing his daughters could do except to try to make the best of it, and try to please the new head of the family as best they could. It warmed my heart when I learned of the courts' decision, because I knew that Donald would finally receive the respect and warm affections of his sisters, which was long deserved and far overdue.

I understand how some members of certain radical, leftist fringe groups think that the patriarchal family model is outdated and idiotic and non-inclusive, and that it is perpetuated by weak- minded, bigoted, senseless, pathetic individuals with delusions that are driven by subconscious weaknesses, but, as I and my fans know, that is not true. We know that our wisest of the wise, the "Man in the Sky" who lives among the clouds, entrusted us with continuing his plan of male dominance, and so we do. Yes, the cost to us is at times very high, yet we willingly suffer the slings and arrows of the non-believers in order to live the proper lives of real men.

Fritz Khrump of course turned out to be completely correct. Donald's business adventures soon caught the attention of world- class investors in all the kingdoms. Everyone in his father's professional circle marveled at his unique style and original methodology. I was told by a reputable source that, while attending a charitable fundraising black-tie event, my source had overheard a group of Donald's closest business associates trumpeting Donald's amazing success. A few examples of the quotes he relayed to me were, "Never in my life have I ever seen anything like this. My God, how much money does that family have?" Another, which obviously refers to how badly Fritz would have wanted to be a part of Donald's brilliant investing plans, was "I think Fritz would roll over twice in his grave and then bust out and crawl his way up through the dirt if he knew what his son was doing with the family fortune." Such obvious admiration and respect and, perhaps, just a little bit of jealousy.

Personally, I consider myself more a spectacular newsman

than a businessman, yet I know my way around the business world, and I certainly know true business genius when I see it. One fantastic example was when, a few years ago, Donald decided to make a bold move far out in front of everyone else in a market sector that had been, up until that time, mostly ignored.

It's the time when he swooped in and cornered the market in extreme high-end solid twenty-four-karat gold kitchen and bathroom fixtures. Donald didn't go the traditional route of buying up shares in companies who produced those products. No, that would have been too common a strategy. Donald decided to go the extra daring mile and buy up all the actual fixtures themselves. Such a visionary! Mountains of sinks, faucets, flexible hoses, soap dispensers, toilets, toilet seats, toilet paper dispensers, toilet bowl plungers, even toilet bowl scrubbers filled his warehouses. If it was made of twenty-four-karat solid gold and it belonged in either a kitchen or bathroom, he bought it. All of it. Every single piece.

While the cost for each piece was much more than the spot gold price, that wasn't important. What was important was to buy early and to buy deep. When there wasn't any inventory left to buy, he began placing custom orders for specialty items: gold toothbrushes, drinking cups, plates, knives, forks, spoons, napkin dispensers, even bathroom curtains made with spun twenty-four- karat gold thread. When he had spent all the family fortune, he borrowed more. He knew that with the world economy steaming along the way it was, it would only be a matter of time before all citizens throughout every kingdom would be clamoring to have those items in their homes. Donald, an amazing genius, was so very far ahead of his time. I remember it as a time when everyone was saying, "That Donald, what a genius."

The crash was completely unexpected. Not one respected

economics professional saw it coming. Everyone was caught off guard, including Donald. It was the largest stock market crash in modern times. The financial industries were rocked to their cores, and the resultant shockwaves brought down all manner of economic sectors with them. This meant the market for high-end luxury goods was gone. Gone for a long, long time. Donald had, through no fault of his own, became a victim of the economy. Incredible potential in such a budding genius entrepreneur was instantly and completely wiped out. Poor Donald was devastated. What promise could his future hold now? For Donald, it seemed the end of his world, and for the next two years, it was.

Perhaps the most extreme depression ever experienced by any individual in the history of the world was the nearly two-year- long depression experienced by our beloved future King Donald. The good doctors at the esteemed Nootztyuu Asylum in the city of Vladd, Pruska had finally reached the limits of their professional knowledge. The world-class reputation of the doctors was the reason why Donald was back in Pruska, and yet sadly, Donald had been unresponsive to all treatments. Two long years of best- in-class treatments for depression was a lot for our future king to endure, and yet, desperate for a cure, he bravely carried on. Sadly, Donald's emotional future seemed hopeless.

Miraculously, one day, Donald's stars finally began to align. That was the day Donald met his future wife and queen, Ninatina. At that time, Ninatina was simply a neatly dressed asylum nurses' helper, a sort of Pruskan candy striper equivalent, who worked helping patients in Donald's ward with, among other things, the maintenance of their basic bodily functions. Ninatina was often complimented by the patients in the ward because of her sweetness, her loving compassion, and her willingness to listen to their hopes and fears, while at the same time helping them to fill out their daily meals menu selection cards. She was much much much younger than Donald, and was such a fantastic beauty, in contrast to Donald, with his orange leathery skin and beady little eyes, and yet, due to some miracle from our "Man Upstairs," they would one day become man and wife.

Ninatina had worked in the ward for many months, and she and Donald were familiar with each other, and yet nothing had ever happened--at least, not until that fateful day. From what I've been told by a very reliable source, one day Ninatina, while sitting on a sturdy metal chair next to Donald's bed, had asked Donald if he would like some extra bacon with his poached eggs for breakfast. Donald looked up from his picture book (my source could not recall the name of the book) responded with an enthusiastic "Yes!," and then asked, "Can I have extra butter on my toast as well?" to which Ninatina responded "Yes, of course you can. If you know how to ask for something, you can always have whatever your little heart desires."

My source told me Donald's sullen mood changed instantly at that very moment. Gone was the sad quiet mumbling moodiness. In its place, my source told me, was a huge gorilla grin--that same crooked gorilla grin that we, his fans and subjects, know and love so well. Somewhere between the bacon and the butter, Donald came to understand the mysteries of the universe, and, because Ninatina was the one who had pulled back the curtain, Donald saw her as an angel and fell in love. I'll admit it sounds like something out of a famous classic novel or an Academy Award-winning film, but no, this was the real deal.

For nearly his entire time in the ward, Donald had spoken

only rarely, and when he did, it was only with the doctors. Now, however, Donald could simply not contain himself. He seemed to feel a level of energy he had not felt since before the market collapsed.

With such amazing energy filling his spirit, Donald set his book to the side and began to speak more. First he asked if he could have a bigger mug for coffee, along with some extra sugar and extra cream. Then, with another burst of energy, he sat up, turned to face her, looked her straight in the eyes, and boldly proclaimed, "I will be someone. Believe me, I will be someone. I will be amazing. You can trust me on that."

Ninatina, not knowing how to respond, looked at him with a confused look and mumbled, "Um, okay."

Donald had to have Ninatina. He needed her badly. My source told me that for the next five minutes our passionate future King Donald told her about his life and dreams. He told her about his family and connections, how he would be great and amazing, and how he would do it all on his own. He told her he would take back his life and what was his, and then promised he would never be made a victim again. He explained how those who had made him a victim would pay, and promised her they would pay big. Donald explained how the name "Khrump" was a symbol of power, and how the bankers, the financiers, and the real estate moguls would all regret having let him down. He told her how his daddy Fritz had worked so hard and for so many years to make the Khrump name an important, respected name, and that he now understood how to take what was his and how to cash in on his daddy's hard work and integrity.

My source told me Donald sat there silent and satisfied for a few moments before telling her "We're going home together."

As incredible as it may seem, Ninatina wasn't quite convinced yet, so Donald seized the moment and showed off his fantastic Khrump family warmth and charm by explaining his "trump card."

He narrowed his eyes in concentration as he suggested to her, "If it would help you to decide, I suppose I could get my favorite Uncle Pootypoo, or King Andre as you people around here like to call him, to give me a glowing recommendation," as he smiled his famous gorilla grin. Wow, can you imagine? Who could possibly resist that kind of charm?

Now came a key moment in both their lives. My source explained that Ninatina turned and looked around the ward, from the electroshock table and generator with its myriad groupings of wires that seemed to grow out from all sides, to the rows of empty beds where the journalists had been, but were now empty, to the tall stack of shiny bedpans still needing to be cleaned in the corner of the room near the giant oversized sink, to the rows of beds with so many patients all waiting their turn for her attention.

She turned back to Donald, with his beady little anticipating eyes, burning red with want and so much love, sighed and said softly, "Yes sir, I'll get my things." Readers, if that ain't love, ain't nothin' love! Ninatina, such a classy lady, could certainly teach our women here a thing or two about love and respect, right? They are one classy couple!

Over the next three years, Donald built up an absolute fortune with ingenuity, class, and hard work--perhaps some of the hardest work ever done by a human being. With leadership and vision, he spread his famous Khrump name like wildfire, and it was soon seen everywhere! Branding became Donald's middle name. Not really, but it should have. Businesses from around the world were vying for a simple way to impress their clientele, and they found it with the Khrump brand, which offered a store-bought instant implied integrity. Donald loved his father very much, and as such he knew that the best way to honor his father's lifetime legacy would be by cashing in. If a fancy new casino, an expensive high-end hotel, or a PGA-level golf course decided they wanted a piece of the pie, Donald was only too happy to serve it up, but it would come at a very high price. There were times, however, when Donald would graciously allow the Khrump name to be licensed for different less prestigious projects, such as common household cleaning product lines. He wisely saw this as a way to keep in touch with what he considered the simple lower-class common people.

Donald even boldly decided to start his own line of household products. We're all of course familiar with the famous Khrump trash and garbage bags, and the television ads with the slogan "If you think trash, think Khrump!" Our charitable future King Donald even insisted that the company give away one free professional golf lesson to one lucky child for every ten million bags sold. By the way, if by this time there's still someone who isn't convinced of Donald's deep understanding of the concerns of the common working-class folks, then I suppose that there's nothing he could ever do that would convince them. Sad.

After years of wonderful successes, something happened that helped to bring Donald further along in his journey to becoming our beloved King. An opportunity. A golden opportunity. A solid twenty-four-karat golden opportunity. At the time, Donald and his financial exploits were being featured nearly daily in all the mainstream newspapers as well as the less-reputable tabloids. The story of his meteoric rise through the ranks of the world's wealthiest individuals, as well as the details of his personal life, all became news for daily public consumption. Donald loved the constant attention, but his relationship with Ninatina began to suffer because of the complete lack of privacy brought on by the incessant prying by the media for every detail of their daily lives. Ninatina, having decided that she had had enough, departed the Khrump family compound and headed home to Pruska for a few months of peace and quiet, although we all know now that she extended that few months to a full year.

One week later, after she had left, poor Donald, feeling so frustrated and alone with only the constant attention of the media at his side, began to pray to our "Man in the Sky." Seeking a new purpose, and unsure of what direction his life should take, Donald prayed for guidance on how best to use his myriad talents, boundless energy, and amazing good looks. Donald selflessly instructed the "Man in the Sky" to use him in a way in which he, Donald, could best help the world. Every evening, as our brilliant dynamic future King Donald, so sad and confused, drifted off to sleep, he questioned if the "Ultimate Intelligence" knew what it was doing. After all, how could someone like himself, so wondrous and unique, not be used for an ultimate glorious purpose? Little did Donald know that one part of the answer, as well as the next part of his journey, would be revealed very soon.

I know about that time in his life because one time, while Donald and I were enjoying an afternoon show in a gentlemen's club, he confided in me about that painful time in his life. It was a very special afternoon that I'll always remember. We would have talked even more that afternoon, except that Brandi Bubbles was about to come on stage.

Anyway, a few days passed, and Donald decided to host a summer party at the Khrump family compound. He invited some friends over, and one of his friends brought a special guest. The guests name was Yogi Bannen, and he was hoping to talk with Donald. Yogi was a producer/director who usually specialized in conspiracy films, but that week a studio executive had called him with an offer for a television show. Pseudo Reality television shows were becoming very popular at that time, and, although when the project was first offered to him he blanched at the idea of being involved, after negotiating some small changes to the basic premise, he was satisfied enough and so agreed to take on the project.

The original premise was to be a satirical look at executive bosses. The plan was to have a funny animal--perhaps a grizzly bear, or even a pot-bellied pig--be dressed up as an executive boss who would challenge a group of interns to put together their best individual plans in order to compete with each other in various business challenges. The interns would be competing for the next open spot on an executive advisory board. Extensive use of overdubbing would have obviously been used for the main character, and the show would have followed a preset script, which would have included the results of the competition. The actual winning intern was to be chosen based on the level of believability that the intern had been able to project into the show. The revised premise kept much of the original premise, with one big change being that more realism be given to the role of the executive boss. Yogi absolutely insisted upon this. Unfortunately, after weeks of auditions for the lead executive boss role proved to be fruitless, Yogi, who had heard so much about Donald, wondered if it would be possible to contact him and ask him to play the part of the executive boss. Luckily for Yogi, a close friend of his was an entertainment reporter at one of the major tabloids, whose assignment at the time had been to interview

Donald on a nearly daily basis. He happened to mention to Yogi that there was going to be a party at the Khrump family compound, so Yogi asked if he could tag along.

By the way, I'm sure you've guessed that the name of the show was the now legendary *How to Monkey Your Way to the Top*, Donald's award-winning television debut. On that evening, when asked to join the show's cast, Donald jumped at the chance. Yes, Donald absolutely loved the idea of performing, as well as the opportunity to expand his contacts list to include so many from the Hollywood entertainment industry. He also realized the show might allow him to accelerate the growth of his celebrity businessman status--which, by the way, it certainly did.

Donald enjoyed that time of his life tremendously, and, for a while, it seemed as if his career as a prime-time reality show actor would continue far into the future. The show enjoyed several wonderfully successful seasons until one day something completely unexpected happened, which caused our future king to change direction and take the next huge step in his journey.

Donald was a guest on the Spanish-language late night talk show Tarde en la Noche. He was there to promote the "mustwatch" season's last episode of his amazing show. Our beloved Donald, always a sport, was sitting in the chair next to the host Esteban Colberto, trying desperately to understand what Colberto was saying. Colberto was famous for liking to poke fun at his guests, and on that night he was holding nothing back. It was an uncomfortable evening for Donald, who just sat there completely silent. Sure, I'll admit that Esteban was somewhat gracious to be conversing with Donald in English, yet it was obvious it didn't matter. As all good kingdom citizens are aware of, it's almost impossible to understand those people when they start speaking our good language with that cheap accent.

Everyone could see that Donald was becoming visibly upset as he fidgeted in his chair. We've all been in that situation. He was obviously imagining all the terrible things that the host was most likely saying about him. We could all see that the evening obviously wasn't going well, especially when Esteban stopped talking and just stared at Donald. Someone in the camera booth must have decided they had to do something, because that's when the strange little guy in the bumblebee costume came running out from behind the curtain, grabbed a tricycle prop, and rode it out into the audience like a complete lunatic. Wow, those ethnic people just love craziness and confusion.

Poor Donald just sat there in continued agitated silence. Esteban must have thought the show was back on track, because that's when the zoo keeper with the tiny monkey on his shoulder came out from behind the curtain, walked over, and sat down next to Donald. Over the next few minutes, all sorts of strange ethnic insanity broke loose. Dancing girls with no dancing talent, but with such amazing bodies came out from back stage and started jumping around and tossing what looked like shiny Christmas tree tinsel all over poor Donald. Next, a bunch of kids came running out of the audience, with two of them riding on the back of a huge pig! The whole time this was going on, that horrible cha-cha music was blaring from the sound system, and as if that wasn't bad enough, everyone in the audience was laughing and singing as loud as they could! Talk about complete and total insanity! It was pretty much a set-up for what happened next!

Now, if you consider how understandably tired and confused poor Donald was by then, then it doesn't really come as a big surprise that Donald jumped up and ran after that little girl who had been invited to come up from out of the audience to pet the tiny zoo monkey. Besides, everyone knows how fast Donald can move, so believe me, if he had really wanted to catch that cute little ten-year-old girl, he certainly could have. Heck, what normal man wouldn't have been affected by all the beautiful girls on the stage anyway, right? Also, I'll be the first one to admit that Donald may have overreacted a little when he bit that tiny monkey in half, but, seeing as the monkey did bite him first, I do think it was a fair response.

Come on, people, it was a show! Donald is a showman! He couldn't help himself! He just did what came naturally to him! He was playing to the crowd! What came next was just pure showman entertainment genius, and nothing less than what I've come to expect! Seizing the moment, Donald jumped up onto Esteban's desk, clenched his full-sized man hands above his head and screamed into the cameras, "You wait and see, you greasy brown scummy bastards! I'll be elected king and I'll make sure we haul all your nasty, dirty brown asses back to the Middle and Central Kingdoms, you wetback sleazy scum!"

Now, again, we all know it just was part of the show! Donald really knows how to have fun with unexpected satire! Such an incredible showman! Sure, if taken out of context, without regard to the fact that it was all in good fun, that quote could almost be seen to be some kind of over-the-top racial slur. Yet we, his faithful subjects who love, understand, and respect our loving leader, know that he doesn't have a racial discrimination bone in his body. If you, my reader, unfortunately happen to know someone who has lingering doubts about our beloved King Donald's character, please tell them they can take it from me, Phil O. Reilly, that it was all done for entertainment, because if there's something I know about, it's racism. I and my colleagues at Fix News know racism very well. You might even say we know it better than anyone else in the news world. You might even say it's our middle name--but no, it's not. Yet it should be, because we at Fix News have what I call "an intimate relationship with the word."

Now, certainly nobody ever expected for Donald to make good on his promise and actually compete to be elected king of our great country, and yet, the very next day, Donald, brilliantly seizing on the incredibly high ratings from his previous night's performance, announced at an afternoon news conference held at the Khrump family compound his candidacy for the kingship as a Repugnican. This took the Repugnican National Committee completely by surprise and yet, within a few days, it became boldly apparent to the RNC leaders that Donald was exactly the sort of energetic king our beloved kingdom was in need of. At that time, our King Chezvic Dandyfoyl was in desperate need of forced retirement after so many years of a so-called "return to prosperity." We needed someone exciting with amazing fresh ideas on how to bring us back to actual prosperity, where the wealthiest citizens of our kingdom would finally have their just due. At that time, my friends and I of the top ten percent had suffered for so many years with a ridiculously anemic annual income growth of only twelve to twenty percent! It was the absolute height of unfairness! I, my family, my friends, and my associates had graciously taken on the role of being the ultimate guardians of civilization, and yet what did we ever get for such a sacrifice? Years and years of grotesquely unfair economic policies! Finally, someone would bring back the love and respect we deserved for our heroic stewardship over the common man. The one, the only, the Donald.

It's hard to believe, but not everyone could understand the importance of having someone as amazing as Donald Khrump as our leader. The Dreamocratic National Committee unfortunately had its own terribly weak-minded idea of who would be best suited to lead us. They nominated Rodina Hilton, and by doing so, created the necessity for a tedious boring debate and then an election, thereby delaying our glorious future. Of course, the Repugnicans could have simply taken over the government by force. While that was of course always an option, the election victory did add to its legitimacy, so with all things considered, it was obviously worth the wait.

The Debate

The debate was an elegant affair hosted by the Noble Land Performing Arts Center in our kingdom's capital, Arguetonia. It was a fitting choice for the debate, given Donald's status as a popular television celebrity. I was there in an official capacity to cover the debate for Fix News, along with my beautiful co-anchor Hanna Seanity. I'll admit I screamed like a teenage schoolgirl when Donald first came out on the stage, but it was nothing compared with my co-anchor, who cried and screamed like a banshee, and, I found out later, even peed a bit into her little pink polka-dot panties. A lesser man might have felt jealous, but, being a real man, I completely understood her reaction.

A few moments later, Rodina came out, and, in keeping with the fun-loving, competitive spirit of the event, we of course booed and spit at her. After the moderator had explained the rules, a coin was tossed, the Repugnicans won, and Donald began speaking. He roared straight ahead with his plans for making the kingdom safe again from the fringe elements, being sure to back up his opinions with valuable statistical data when suddenly, after less than two minutes,

Rodina interrupted him by asking where he had gotten his information, rudely implying it may have been inaccurate. Well, after she got away with that infant-like behavior the first time, there was no stopping her. Shortly afterward, she did it again, and again, and again. She seemed absolutely intent on not allowing Donald to finish explaining his plan.

After the third interruption, Donald, rightfully so, became irritated and said to her, "Shut up and sit down, you nasty scumpig!" to the delight of the Repugnican supporters. The childish horrified reaction from the Dreamocrats was so unexpected that you would almost think they had never been to a debate before. Huge shouts of criticism were coming from the Dreamocrats' side of the audience, so Donald turned to them and shouted, "She is such a nasty woman! It's an abomination when females like her don't accept their place in the grand scheme of things and refuse to show subservience to males. I'd like to just go over to her right now and give her a good beating and rip her throat out!"

Now, of course, on the surface that might have seemed rude or crude, or perhaps something of a dangerous threat, but to us Repugnicans, we knew it was just our energetic showman Donald showing us his good old-fashioned values, as well as making good TV even better--plus, we understood he was just letting loose and having some fun with the audience. I just shook my head in disbelief when I saw how the Dreamocrat nut cases had taken his comments to heart, with some of them calling his behavior dangerous. Others even went so far as to say he was sexist and cruel and uncultured and pathetic. I even heard someone yell out that he was a coward! Yes, it's hard to believe, but it did actually happen. Luckily, there were also members of the crowd who were perfectly sane. Myself, my family, my friends, my business associates, and of course every Repugnican there saw him for what he was: a breath of fresh air. Sure, he may have lacked a certain level of sophistication, but wow, was he exciting!

A little while later, while Rodina was preaching and going on and on about fairness and equality and clean water and nature and puppies and blah blah blah, Donald moved a little closer to be able to hear her better. Unfortunately, he tripped on a wrinkle in the carpet and nearly fell over, accidentally kicking Rodina in her side as he tried to catch his balance. It was obviously a total accident, but you wouldn't have known it by the loud and ridiculous commotion the Dreamocrats made. There was a short break, after which "creampuff" Rodina was back on her feet.

I could see she was obviously feeling some kind of childish need to punish Donald for accidentally kicking her. She started off by telling the audience that Donald didn't have real factual opinions about anything because he didn't have the patience to read, and it wouldn't matter if he did bother to read because the important information he should have been reading wasn't published in a picture book format anyway.

Next, she said that having Donald in a position of power was like having an insane insecure screaming monkey in charge of a weapons supply depot while holding a can of gasoline, a lit flamethrower, and a hand grenade with the pin pulled. I'll admit that the picture she painted for her supporters did have some humor to it, but we, Donald's loyal supporters, knew the image was off the mark.

For the remainder of the debate, it was back and forth, back and forth. Rodina continually tried to fill the debate with her hate and terrible lies, yet thankfully, despite her best efforts to cut him down, Donald was still able to rise above it all and shine like the northern star on a cool clear night. Perhaps one day the Dreamocrats will be able to let go of their high and mighty so-called "ideals" and join the rest of us in our celebration of who we are right now instead of who we could be. Perhaps they'll understand that Donald's appeal comes not only from shared subconscious insecurities and an exaggerated fear of the unknown, but also from the common desire to have whatever one wants whenever one wants it. Donald and we, the top ten percenters, have always had that privileged sort of life, and the middle and lower classes of course hope that by being associated with us, they might also someday be able to have the same privileges. We are the shepherds and they are the sheep who lovingly follow along. What came next? He killed her! In the election results, of course.

THE FIRST 100 DAYS
NOVEMBER 9
Day One: The Coronation

That first day, and what a fittingly beautiful day for Donald's coronation! With a flair for the dramatic, Donald came galloping into the courtyard of the palace riding hard on his young but well-broken-in gelding Pollyryann. Dragging along behind him on a very sturdy but worn fifty-foot length of rope was Rodina Hilton. Donald and Rodina had decided to show the citizens of the kingdom their solidarity in a fun and creative way by making it look as if she was a prisoner and Donald was a conquering hero. They even went so far as to have a pair of guards untie her and take her into the main building along with an announcement that she would be spending a little time away. I'll admit that their show was becoming a little tedious when they had the fake ambulances arrive and carry her out on a stretcher, but after all, it was just good harmless entertainment for the Repugnicans who were there to observe their Donald's coronation.

There must have been at least five hundred people there! I don't remember the last time I saw so many citizens show up for a coronation, except perhaps for the coronation of our previous King Chezvic Dandyfoyl when he was elected for the first time. As I'm sure my readers remember, King Dandyfoyl was very popular among the laziest citizens of the kingdom, and most of his followers were irresponsible people who couldn't be bothered to find a job and actually do work. They were there that day simply because there was nothing else for them to do on Coronation Day anyway. Plus, Dandyfoyl had given a press conference prior to the event during which he announced that there would be a super spectacular buffet provided for everyone there that day. It was a humiliating and shameful day for the kingdom. Donald's supporters, in contrast, are very different types of citizens. His supporters who had come out had chosen to sacrifice precious time out of their busy work days in order to come and celebrate their solidarity with their new king. Those supporters who were not there chose to show their affections for the new king by heroically staying at work and on the job.

After the ambulances left and the cheering quieted down a bit, the official coronation ceremony began. I'm not much on kingdom ceremonies, but I'll admit that after his official crowning, it was an amazing spectacle to watch as Donald, in his flowing red crushed-velvet cape with his massive twenty-four-karat solid-gold crown, sauntered down the red-carpeted catwalk toward the podium. Such amazing style and grace! Incredible to watch! When he reached the podium, he began his speech but had to stop and wait because the crowd simply wouldn't quiet down. Such amazing energy was in the air! It was a full five minutes of chanting and cheering, and then, finally, he was able to begin. And what a speech! Even I, Phil O. Reilly, hardened entertainment newsman professional, had to force back a tear as I heard his gripping heartfelt words. Lincoln had his Gettysburg Address, and on that day, equal in glory, Donald had his Coronation Day speech. Sure, Donald's speech was a lot shorter in comparison to Lincoln's, plus Lincoln had spent quite a few hours crafting his, whereas Donald's was "off the cuff," and not written down, yet we could all feel the magic that was happening that day in the kingdom courtyard.

As he wrapped things up near the end of the most amazing three-minute speech ever given, Donald showed his unparalleled generosity when he announced that, due to the huge but smaller than expected citizen turnout, the good folks over at the Official Kingdom Court Royal Golf Course would be receiving the entire unused celebration buffet in order to feed the unfortunate hungry club members who had been unable to attend the coronation ceremony. He also announced that the trusted Fix News Network--yes, my network--would be the one and only network whose reporters would be allowed into the official Royal Kingdom press release events. I believe he did this because he felt that only the Fix News Network, with the kingdom's most professional and reputable news staffers, was suitable for his administration's special needs. Why? Because he felt that the hard working reporters at Fix News were the kinds of professionals who not only understood how to serve him and his staffs needs and desires, but also understood the importance of his administration's selective editing policy. We at the network understood how being chosen by Donald for such an important responsibility was the same as being chosen by the great "Man in the Clouds" for an ultimate holy task. Donald knew that Fix News would never let him or his staff down.

Day Two

Only two days in, and already so many exciting events had begun to unfold in this, the Era of Khrump. The first Official Kingdom Press Release Event was held just outside the Kingdom Court Royal Golf Course. It was a relaxed meeting, and I and my Fix News coworkers were invited to sit on the pavement which was just outside the grassy area which was just outside of the newly built knee-high brick wall area that surrounded the new flower beds. What a beautifully designed flower bed! Whoever the designer was certainly knew what he was doing! He thought of everything! There was even an enormous awning installed to protect the more delicate flowers from the burning afternoon sun. After just a few short hours of waiting, the event began. Our beloved king was busy inside the main building at the time conducting important official court business, so he sent out his official court mascot, John Spice, or as Donald affectionately likes to call him, "Khrump Spice."

John read the press release given to him and then answered reporters' questions. His nickname "Khrump Spice," by the way, came about in part because King Donald had instructed John to read the press release in a powerful "Donald" style. I know this because Donald told me a little story about this just a few hours before in a short exclusive telephone interview. He told me, "I want him to make it sound and feel as if it's actually me standing there reading the release. He has to be me. He has to put me into himself, and you know, as I was watching him practice earlier, he was really doing it! For me, it felt as if I had taken a shaker full of myself and had shaken it all over him, completely covering the little guy. John Spice was doing me good, really good. Amazing!"

John was so good, in fact, that after that first day of reading the press release, as he stood there brimming with confidence, he said to us, "I'll take your questions, but only if you address me as 'Khrump Spice.'"

That, my friends, is teamwork. I and my Fix News associates stood there in amazement. "Questions?" we asked ourselves. "No need for anything of the sort!" I said out loud. "That was amazing!"

Everyone nodded and chortled in agreement.

The amazing press release he read to us during that first event was very important. It contained three short and bold proclamations of Donald's intentions to improve the security of our sacred kingdom, and the following is a summary of the three.

The first concerned the "brownies." "Brownies" have always been welcome in our kingdom, of course, and we have always appreciated the basic but necessary work they have done for us. With that said, we all know that, at times, some of them start to think they are as deserving as the true legitimate citizens who have been born here, and well, we all know that just isn't right. Our wise King Donald decided that it was time to pause their access to privileges in our precious kingdom for a short while. Donald kindly suggested building some vacation camps to allow a little off-work time during which they could perhaps reflect on their good fortune. The vacation camps would be a fun time of reflection for whole families, especially considering there would be no school provided for the kids, which in turn would mean no dreaded homework for them as well. Just good relaxing fun for the entire family. To ensure that they understood they were indeed important valued members of our kingdom, Donald even suggested that they should show their appreciation by helping out with the cost of their stay there, as well as with the cost of the upgrading and expansion of the camps. If it was to happen that a single or group of "brownies" were found to be unfit for the camps, it was possible they might be returned to their home kingdoms for a short stay, during which it was hoped they would contemplate their attitude towards our kingdom's better citizens, after which there would be a possibility for re-entry back into our kingdom at a later date. Donald even graciously suggested that the younger children in the camps, in particular the younger girls, be allowed to stay in the main building of the main palace in order to serve as helpers for the building's staff. In exchange for their labor, the children would receive free specialized training which would guarantee them a brighter future! Imagine that! A golden opportunity and at no cost to their family! The parents of those children would of course be encouraged to leave the kingdom temporarily in order to allow the children in the program to better learn their specialized training without the distraction of family responsibilities.

The second proclamation concerned the "scarfheads." The "scarfheads," as most people know, came from a strange far, far- away kingdom. I've never been there myself, but I'm sure their kingdom is very cold most of the time, and I assume very dusty as well, judging from the way they seem to have an almost religious need to always have their scarves wrapped tightly around their heads, and, oddly enough, sometimes even their whole bodies.

Well, we all know there have been times when the

kingdom's weather has been less than perfect, but it's never meant that we've needed to wear our scarves for the entire day and night, as well as indoors where the temperature was just fine. It was because of such unreasonable, unbalanced thinking that Donald knew he needed to set some new rules in place in regard to when a scarf could be worn. In times of cold weather, scarf-wearing would of course be permitted. In times of warm weather, however, scarf-wearing would be prohibited, and lastly, indoor scarf-wearing would be strictly prohibited during all times of the year.

Even with such basic commonsense guidance being put forth by our great King Donald, I knew what would be coming once the Dreamocrats learned of the restrictions. The Dreamocrats would cry foul about how unfair it was for the government to try to control individual clothing choices. It's sad, really, because Dreamocrats always feel a need for a "cause." I suppose it makes them feel as if they are good people. Luckily for our kingdom, however, King Donald, being a Repugnican, has a much more refined understanding of social issues, and, because of that, he feels no such need.

Next, King Donald informed us that because our kingdom's yearly quota of "scarfheads" had been met, there would be no more permitted to enter for a short time. He also announced a new and exciting program where certain "scarfheads" or groups of "scarfheads" would be moved to special campgrounds. These campgrounds would be of a different variety than the type that the "brownies" would have. Nothing too radical, he promised, just specialized camps that would fit our kingdom's unique needs. Donald wisely pointed out that the key to knowing a person's true self is to give them a verbal test of some kind while under some sort of stress, and those camps would do just that. They would actually be more like specialty questionnaire centers, and would have specially trained people who would run them. Donald lovingly assured the "scarfhead" population that this was only being done to remove the threat of the most dangerous "scarfheads" who might be living among them in their communities. He also suggested that the best way for the "scarfheads" to show their pride in the kingdom would be by sharing in the expenses for the maintenance and potential expansion of the camps in the same way that the brownies were going to. It was a wonderful plan because, after all, we are all in this together.

Still, I knew that when the Dreamocrats found out, they would try to interfere with good sound government policy again. They would of course passionately cite all sorts of studies and statistical information about how wonderful and intelligent and normal and good the "scarfheads" are. They would drone on and on, and then try to claim that we are all the same on the inside, blah, blah, blah, blah, blah. They would probably even have actual statistical data showing how the average "scarfhead" was actually much less likely to commit a crime when compared to a citizen who had been born and raised here. I'd bet they could even show how scarfheads earned advanced degrees at a much higher rate than the average kingdom citizens do, and then they'd try to convince us of how much the "scarfhead" culture added to our kingdoms culture with their rich heritage.

Sorry Dreamocrats, no sale. If you, my reader, are like me, your common sense tells you that anyone who wears a scarf in warm weather just might have a screw loose. Scarfheads have been known to become pretty angry if you walk up to one and try to take their scarf away. Anyone with a brain knows those people are dangerous.

The third proclamation had to do with improving voter registration rules. An overhaul of the rules had been long overdue, and King Donald decided to boldly meet the issue head on. It isn't often that the Dreamocrats rally around a Repugnican idea, but this time I expect they will, seeing as the proclamation is all about fair treatment for everyone.

I'm a card-carrying Repugnican, but I do respect the Dreamocrats. I also admit that most of the time the Dreamocrats do mean well. They do. The problem is that the "ideals" center in a Dreamocrat brain is defective. It's not their fault; they're just born like that. I read about it on a Fix News affiliate website, so you know you can accept it as a verified fact. Sure, some Dreamocrats might object to what I've just written, but the fact that they cannot accept even a simple commonsense idea about their own obviously demented perspective is proof in and of itself that they are unable to see and understand antisocial personality defects. Again, it's not their fault, it's just the way they are.

Sadly, their mental defects affect not only themselves but also all of us in the kingdom. King Donald thankfully had a solution; voter registration testing. New voter registration rules would now require applicants to undergo rigorous psychological testing to ensure that only the most mentally balanced individuals would receive the privilege to vote. It was an excellent idea, seeing as no kingdom on earth allowed mentally deranged citizens to vote. King Donald explained how he and a panel of mental health experts had developed new tests which would be used to screen voters beginning in just a few weeks.

Even better news was when he explained that the tests would assess not only the individual's present degree of mental normalcy, but they would also be able to predict whether the individual has the potential for future mental derangement as well! Amazing! After only one day as king, Donald and his new official kingdom psychiatric staff members had already outdone themselves.

Day Five

After four beautiful days of long-awaited progress, the Dreamocrats, awash in sour grapes, felt the need to start up their rumor mill, and seemed to have it running at full speed. Lies, lies, and more lies, all aimed at smearing King Donald's good character. They should have been ashamed of themselves.

The AVN Network, (The Dreamocrats so-called Actual Verified News Network), began Day Five with the most insane of insane stories involving our good king and his administration. They attacked him viciously and claimed that our chosen leader had more than friendly ties to the kingdom of Pruska and his long- time friend King Andre Putenski. The AVN Network even claimed that they had actual evidence showing that the Pruskan Kingdom had interfered with our election.

During one of their early-morning news talk shows, they paraded all sorts of so-called "evidence" in front of their innocent viewers. First, they showed a two-minute video of someone claiming to be a Pruskan computer hacker describing how he was able to hack the electronic ballot boxes with a sophisticated program. Afterwards, another individual presented a cell phone video that seemed to show our kingdom's traditional paper ballot boxes from key competitive districts being loaded onto trucks, driven to a landfill, dumped into deep trenches, burned, and then covered up with dirt. The only language to be heard in the entire video was the Pruskan language. Talk about ridiculous! If the "evidence" had even the slightest most remote chance of being authentic, I would have been the first one to say so, but seeing as it was all so obviously fake, I won't even dignify their claim with a response. Shame on you, AVN!

Day Six

More outrageous claims from the AVN News Network! One of my colleagues called me earlier in the day and told me to check out the AVN. I clicked on their channel to see what he was talking about, and to me, it looked as if one of their reporters had gone down to the local landfill and had filled the trunk of a car with boxes of junk. They were broadcasting from the parking area just out in front of their main building. Their star reporter Kent Toppel was bent over peering into the trunk of a car that was parked there. Kent was explaining that his network had been contacted by an individual who claimed to have broken into the main warehouse of the Khrump Family Compound and stolen personal items belonging to King Donald. He further explained that he was told the car containing the items had been parked directly in front of the AVN building. In the car's trunk were plastic storage boxes with at least half of the labels smudged and half peeled off. Some of the labels were however readable, and Kent took the opportunity to read a few of them. The first label read "Pruskan blackmail sex tape 14 version B." Another read "Khrump Klassic / Almost Legal," whatever that was supposed to mean.

The first questions that came to my mind, as I'm sure they did to all other law abiding citizens were: "Since when is burglary not a crime? Isn't that the bigger story here?" and "Since when do supposedly reputable reporters associate with criminals?" I saw it as a terribly sad moment for their network, because I had never seen them stoop so incredibly low. Even for them, this represented a new bottom. To have a news network with such an enormous potential for greatness cavorting with criminals and promoting obviously manufactured fake news trash was just too much for someone of my glowing reputation to stand. I found myself hoping that our great and wise King Donald would find a way to make them stop. With King Donald and King Andre having been such good friends for so many years, it seemed an absolute shame if such blatant lies were to create any tension in their close friendship.

I'd read that King Andre had always been one to bend over backwards to do whatever was necessary to ensure the smooth running of his kingdom, so I felt sure he could offer some sage advice to King Donald. Even better than that, I was hoping he'd show King Donald some appropriate techniques to absolutely ensure the AVN Network would show more discretion in the future, and learn how to better decide which stories deserved investigation, and which stories, obviously fake, they should ignore. In keeping with the spirit of the brotherhood of news networks, I humbly suggest the AVN Network could certainly have learned a thing or two from my Fix News Network..

Day Seven

Finally, a response from our great King Donald. After enduring the pain of insulting fake news for days, Donald stepped into the fray and ended the indignity, and he did it in an overwhelmingly classy way. Donald contacted the AVN Network executive owners and invited them and their families to the palace for a closed-door conference. It must have been quite exciting to receive such an invitation, and yet you would have never known it by the look on the attendees' faces. As those ingrates from the AVN Network, along with their family members, were parading into the palace, they looked much more dead than alive.

Personally, I and all my colleagues at Fix News would have been completely thrilled to have received such an invitation, and you can bet we would have been appreciative enough to have shown it with happy smiling faces. I believe our King Donald was aware of this, and I think that was the reason why only Fix News reporters were allowed to be there to cover the event. After just a few short hours, our king's favorite spokesman John "Khrump Spice" came out through the conference room door and walked to the podium to make a formal announcement. He was obviously feeling excited as he began his short statement.

"Our great and amazing King Donald has graciously and selflessly offered to provide a month-long vacation at the Khrump Family Compound, complete with specialized nanny services, for the younger children of the AVN Network executive owners. The Network executives themselves will be spending the next thirty days at an all-expenses-paid campground seminar retreat named 'King Khrump's News Accountability Institute,' where they will relearn the importance of approved integrity in news reporting."

"King Donald planned to have them address you themselves, but they were all so excited about the coming month that they wanted to get started right away. They felt there was no need to tell you this personally, and in fact they asked me to pass the information along to you, which is what I'm doing right now. That concludes todays press release. Unfortunately, there is no time this afternoon to answer reporters' questions due to the multitude of activities we in our king's administration are involved with today."

Honestly, after hearing that, I was feeling a little shocked and perhaps a bit peeved and jealous as well. I thought to myself that perhaps next time I'd be the one to produce fake news if the result was to receive an all-expenses-paid vacation as a punishment. After thinking about it for a little while though, I did begin to appreciate our wise king's decision of wanting to keep all the kingdom's news professionals up to date with the latest and best training. Perhaps we could all learn a thing or two about tolerance from King Donald.

Day Ten

Day Ten of King Donald's reign was perhaps the most spiritual day ever in the history of our great kingdom. I am sure that someday soon it will be made an official kingdom holiday. The largest church in the kingdom, The Church of the Holy Rollers, asked, or perhaps the correct expression would be "begged," our great King Donald to come and sit in on an early-morning mass. The church officials perhaps wanted to show how even a great, important man like our king could still find time for spiritual endeavors. It was to be a simple mass in the lower levels of the church basement, but our king asked if it could be in the main cathedral area instead to allow more church goers to share the day with him as he celebrated our "Man in the Sky."

When King Donald arrived at the church, he was accompanied by his wife Ninatina, and they had with them a large rectangular wrapped package that was to be a gift to the church. Ninatina had not been crowned queen as of yet because Donald, in his wisdom, didn't want to cause unneeded confusion or distraction with another royal ceremony so soon after his own coronation. Just one more example of how King Donald blesses us every day with his pearls of wisdom.

Talk about a full house! Those long bench seats must have had at least thirty worshipers each, and there must have been at least one hundred benches! Quite a crowd! Unfortunately, I wasn't able to be there that day, and had to rely on taped video for my journal. Sadly, my overwhelming work load takes up every day of my week, and I've reluctantly had to sacrifice my church day in order to complete my work duties. I've accepted this, however, because I consider the extra work I do on such a holy day to be a sort of penance I pay to the "Man Upstairs" for the excess beauty of my life. Let me tell you, though, after viewing the tape of that special day, and feeling the amazing spiritual energy coming through the television, I realized just how much I missed by not being there, so I promised myself I would most definitely be there at some time in the future.

The main cathedral area was enormous, and so impressive, with so many colorful stained glass windows and religious portraits surrounding the seating areas. The dizzying height of the vaulted ceiling was decorated in all manner of brightly colored frescos done so long ago, yet still they carried the full weight of the significance of the events they depicted. After just a short time into the mass, our king surprised the church elders when he asked if he could be allowed to speak just a few words to the guests there. Obviously, our King Donald was feeling inspired and needed to say a few words in honor of the holy beauty that was surrounding him. Donald and Ninatina were seated on the front row bench, so it was just a short walk to the main altar. He carried with him the gift he had brought for the church elders. Our King Donald seemed to feel momentarily humbled by the greatness of his surroundings as he stood there quietly looking out over the crowd. Next, he lowered his gaze, most likely for a short prayer, cleared his throat, and again looked out over the crowd. He began to speak.

"Wow!" he said. "Wow, look at this place!" King Donald really does like to show appreciation for the citizens and the things that are important to them, and that was just one more validated example. Our king continued, "First, I'd like to thank the monsignor or the minister or whatever you call him for the chance to speak with all of you here in your place of worship. Most people are not aware of it, but I am a highly religious man and I've always loved the way you people do your worshipping. Beautiful thing really, beautiful. Some of you carry around your special little prayer bead necklaces, and some of you prefer to carry around your tiny little vial of special miracle water, and so on and so on.

"Wow, I think to myself. Wow. You people really believe in this stuff, and that is powerful, very very powerful, and amazing. I think of the market that your water could appeal to if you decided to sell it. There are so many sick people in the kingdom, and I imagine that the ones who can't come and get it themselves would probably be willing to pay almost anything for it. They would practically be begging you for it. You'd really have a market there."

"Well, I didn't come here to give business advice. I get paid to do that, but you can have that one for free. After all, it is a Sunday, and I've heard how much that means to you people. Oh yes, and this is for you. I almost forgot. Here's a little gift for your little church or temple or whatever you call it here. I apologize for the frame being so big, but I had no idea of the sizes of the frames you already had, but bigger is better, so here you go."

Our generous King Donald then quickly unwrapped the gift he had brought and held it up high for all the worshippers to see. It was a gorgeous photocopy of the painting that was done immediately after his coronation. The original was, of course, in the central palace for all visitors to be able to gaze upon during the popular palace tours. It was a beautiful copy in a beautiful gold frame.

King Donald knew he was no interior designer, but being the helpful type he was, he turned around, looked up and down the wall behind him, and then graciously offered his opinion to the crowd for the perfect spot. "Well, if we move that painting of the guy with the thorns on his head—ouch, that must hurt--over to the side wall, then you can have my photo centered on the wall right behind the altar here. I'll just set it here and you can take care of it later. If I could have your attention for a moment more, that would be great. Something of huge importance has come to my attention, and I'd like to ask for your help.

"As you all know, my former television show *How to Monkey Your Way to the Top* has had to do without me for some time now. After I offered my talents to our kingdom, my longtime special friend the former King of Austrinia Arnold Shifenbakker called me and asked for the opportunity to play the role of executive boss on my show. As I'm sure you are all aware of, he sort of blew it. I'm sure you are all as concerned about it as I am, so If you could pray and ask your special "Man in the Sky" to do something for him and my show, I would absolutely totally appreciate it. Also, if you could do something else that might really work, just call the network and tell them how much you like the show, because that would actually help.

"It's a huge favor I ask, and I understand that; however, I am your king, and I would appreciate the favor in a huge way, so please don't let me down. I'll tell you what. All of you do what I said, and I'll make sure that these god houses are always tax free, because, wow, wouldn't it be terrible if your place here had to lose its tax-exempt status? That would be terrible, absolutely terrible and unfair. Hey, look at me, I'm like that guy on the television game show who makes deals for whatever it is that's behind the curtains, right? This is great! Hey, by the way, they told me that this place had really great pancakes! Is that right? At least, that's what I was told."

I could see from the video from that day that King Donald made quite an impression on his audience. Born with an intuitive understanding of the spiritual nature of the common man, Donald truly shone that day. We are all so blessed to have him.

Day Eleven

It should have been a wonderful day, and yet, unfortunately, it wasn't. It's so shameful when a fully grown adult male behaves as if he's an adolescent school girl who has just been dumped by her boyfriend. I'm talking of course about the former Austrinian King Arnold Shifenbakker. One day after the news broke about our King Donald humbly asking the "Man Upstairs" supporters to please help breathe some life into Arnold's sad performance on the show How to Monkey Your Way to the Top, Shifenbakker was out in front of his garish multimillion-dollar mansion speaking to reporters. It was a hastily called press conference at which he furiously denounced our great king, and even more unbelievably, he threatened our loving King Donald with violence!

His exact words were "I want to smash his stupid gorilla face into a table top!" Wow, right? How terrible!

I usually have trouble understanding him when he speaks, as I'm sure most others do, but there was no mistaking what he said that day. I've heard that he seems to believe that he speaks our sacred language very well, but anyone with human ears knows that he obviously does not. That aside, though, he seemed to believe our great king was not entitled to call him out for his terrible performance. He actually seemed to have felt insulted at having been the recipient of so many genuine caring churchgoers' prayers. Can you believe it? That, my friends, was a direct insult to the "Man Upstairs." It's a terrible day when someone in a position of privilege speaks so poorly of the faithful.

As for the show, my friends, I was a faithful watcher of the original show, and I can attest to Donald and his show as having been the most watchable of "must-watch TV." I remember eagerly anticipating the end of each episode when Donald would assess each contestant's performance. Everyone watching would wonder who would stay and who would go? It was always a nail-biter.

Unfortunately, with Shifenbakker replacing Donald as the executive boss on the show, it felt different. I'm sure he was trying, but he seemed to be so uncomfortable in the role right from the start. His character didn't seem to be willing to crush someone's future on a whim the way Donald's did. So sad. Perhaps some of his oversensitivity can be attributed to the massive quantity of strength drugs his kingdom circus had forced him to ingest so many years ago when he was his kingdom's official strongman. I've read before that sometimes the side effects of those drugs can influence an individual's mood even years after stopping use. Perhaps we should ask the "Man in the Clouds" to help Shifenbakker with his future performances by taking away his "sensitive" side and allowing that ice-cold executive side to emerge.

Day Twelve

Luckily for all of us, within a single day, the bromance drama between Donald and Arnold had been resolved. Only a few hours after Shifenbakker's news conference, our king was fast on his way to Austrinia aboard Airplane One. Arnold greeted Donald on the runway shortly after his plane touched down, and, after a brief but vicious impromptu wrestling match--in which our beloved Donald did very well, by the way--their bromance was back on track. Donald stayed the day as a guest at the Shifenbakker mansion, and, when it came time to leave, the two of them had ironed out all their differences.

Day Fifteen

On the fifteenth day of our famously respectable King Donald's reign, The AVN Network clowns came out with yet another fake news story, and this time, it was spectacularly fake. That network really outdid itself this time. Their story relied on a small portion of an old highly confidential sound check recording which had been stolen from the office of esteemed radio talk show host Stanley Howard a few days earlier. The recording was purported to stand as a testament for our king's disrespect for women. As anyone with half a brain knows, any recording can be taken out of context, and that is exactly what the low to no integrity reporters over at AVN did.

On the day of that particular recording, the sound checks were performed just as they had always been for every broadcast. For readers who may not be familiar with the procedures of a radio station, sound checks are done to ensure that all sound equipment and settings are working and set properly. Stanley's obsessive attention to detail for all things, including the sound checks, is one of the many reasons why his show has won so many awards, as well as the admiration and respect from fellow famous personalities like myself. Sure, there are some who think that Stanley's obsessive nature is irritating, and I'm sure there are some others who are put off by his only occasionally washed thick shaggy hair hanging in his face constantly, plus his coke bottle glasses sure don't do much for his looks, but hey, I still like the guy. He may look like a filthy big-city hoarder who secretly has floor-to-ceiling bundles of ancient newspapers along with stacks and stacks of rotting old pizza boxes and half-eaten moldy sandwiches hidden in his squalid closet-sized apartment, but the truth in fact is that it's an unfair characterization of who he is.

How do I know? Because I've known him his whole life, and I've never ever seen him read a newspaper, a magazine, or even a comic book for that matter. Oh, it's not because he can't or that he's unwilling to, it's simply because he likes to live each day in a moment by moment "gut feeling" kind of way, which, by the way, is exactly the way that Donald likes to live as well. Perhaps that's why they're such famously good buddies.

On the night of the taping, he and Donald wanted to have some fun during the sound checks before the show began, so Stanley asked Donald to treat the sound checks as if they were a sort of audio screen test. Instead of the usual "testing testing, can you hear me?" sort of cues, Stanley suggested that Donald come up with a sort of creative monologue about how he might imagine his life if, instead of having only 49% gorilla DNA, he instead had 94% gorilla DNA, plus that he lived in the wilds of the jungle and was in heat. Donald, always a sport, agreed to give it a try.

Well, folks, I'm here to say that he was so spectacular and so believable, that even now, when I hear it, it almost seems real. Donald was simply reading lines he had written on a piece of paper, but wow, he really knocked it out of the park, so to speak. He's one heck of a natural actor, and seeing as he had never had even one day of acting class, that makes it all the more amazing! From what I've heard from the people who were there that day, he even ad libbed like a pro near the end of the recording after he had come to the end of his script. I've included some of the transcription here in order to let my reader understand how it could have been so easily misunderstood.

" ....And when I go up to them, they just want me. It doesn't matter if they work for me or not, I can feel it. I usually let them touch my crotch, and, if they don't want to, I make them anyway because I know they really want to. I know that, and they know that. We all know that. I just whip it out, and they scream with ecstatic joy and can hardly contain themselves. Those little nasty bitches really love it. I can do anything I want because they love it so much. I grab 'em hard by their crotches and squeeze until they scream and beg for me to stop. Damn, they love it so much! Little bitches and teen bitches, but old bitches don't do it for me. I mean, they want it, but I don't. Who wants that old bitch shit, right?"

Of course, after the tape was made public, opportunists

came out of the woodwork trying to cash in on the misunderstanding. By the end of the day, the AVN network claimed that they had in their possession signed sworn statements claiming assault by our king from nineteen women, sixteen teenage girls, ten girls under ten years old, and even five men, all of whom had come in voluntarily to speak to their network staff. Is there no shame anymore? Doesn't anyone believe in honesty and integrity? It was so sad watching their network struggling to force their viewers to believe such nonsense. Very very sad.

King Donald and I have had many conversations before about this exact sort of thing. I personally have had this very same event occur in my own life. It is because of our shared experiences that he and I have come to understand the exact reasons why this occurs. Typically, when an unattractive woman with an unfit body starts feeling unhappy and desperate because of her sadly average little life, she'll begin looking for an opportunity to share her misery, and will typically target a tall, good-looking, hard-working man to ruin, thereby bringing him down to her level where she expects he will eventually want her as a mate. This sad beast of a woman will eventually be convinced to go away, but typically only after receiving some public pity and a few bucks. Unfortunately, because Donald and I are such popular and great-looking men who are also constantly in the public eye, we are both obvious targets for such grossly demented women, and, sadly, this sort of thing is destined to happen to both him and me again and again throughout our entire lives. Such is the price for being such wonderfully attractive and phenomenally wealthy great men.

Sadly, due to the weaker gender's mental softness and mean-spiritedness, they simply cannot stop themselves. They have done this throughout the ages, and are sure to continue.

There is good news, though. I was able to convince our king of the importance of making an example of those who try to besmirch any good man's name, and our great King Donald promised to do just that. He promised a "heads will roll" sort of resolution. So, cheer up good men of the kingdom who may have been accused of assault on a female, because help is on the way. You will suffer no more.

Day Twenty

A wonderful couple of days have passed. Absolutely wonderful and productive also. On day twenty of his reign, King Donald himself, using a solid twenty-four-karat-gold-handled shovel, broke ground in a small ceremony for the two short-term vacation holding camps for the "brownies" and the "scarfheads." Those two initial campgrounds, of what I hope will be the first of many, will be built in the brutally cold and sparsely populated northern region of our kingdom's woodland territories. After the ceremony, during a short speech, he announced to the cheering crowd that it had been a very exciting and productive week, and that the new and long-overdue voter registration changes were nearly ready and in the process of being finalized for trial testing.

He also announced that on the very next day, his legal support staff would be completing the final version of what he considered his best executive decree ever, which he named "The Audio Tape Decree." It would immediately halt the unfair treatment of the kingdom's men by aggressive, unhinged women. He explained that his decree would set up a series of penalties for women who make gross accusations against men, with the full details of his plan coming very soon.

King Donald then made his final announcement, which I thought was perhaps the best announcement of the entire day. The reporters from the AVN Network who were responsible for the fictitious story about the king's alleged victims' assault claims had been rounded up and were all in the process of being shipped off to King Khrump's News Accountability Institute for retraining. Finally, real justice for all had begun.

Day Twenty-Two

Feeling the need for a short break from the responsibilities of transforming our kingdom, King Donald and Ninatina enjoyed a wonderful lunch and some much needed private time together at the kings favorite luncheon restaurant "Leggs & Eggs" located inside the Margo Leggy Country Club in the southeastern city of Floridinia.

Airplane One transported the two of them, along with their sixty-two most-needed staff workers, down to the famous hot spot for a stress-free, delicious lunch. While they dined, they enjoyed the amazingly beautiful view of the coastline from the private VIP club veranda.

After lunch, Mrs. Khrump wisely decided it was time for some feminine upkeep, so she quickly headed off to one of the many stylish boutiques and beauty salons that line the walking paths around the club grounds. If you're like me and our good King Donald, you know that a good woman can never be too feminine or too gently submissive, so it's always best to encourage them when they feel the need to visit the salons for their fancy treatments and upgrades. King Donald, suddenly finding himself with free time and an open schedule, selflessly decided that an impromptu visit to the local children's hospital would be on that day's agenda.

An hour later, with his security staff accompanying him, Donald began a tour of the East Floridinia Children's Hospital. Unfortunately, after just a few minutes into the tour, something very strange happened. An odd man in a white coat with a pinned- on name badge, who was walking slightly bent over and a little tilted to the side, came up to King Donald and began aggressively asking him questions about the new campgrounds that were being built for the "brownies" and the "scarfheads." Poor Donald, caught completely off guard and believing he was about to be attacked, of course defended himself. Yes, it did turn out later that the man in question was a hospital doctor who had a debilitating muscle disease which accounted for his unusual stance, yet unfortunately at the time, there was simply no possible way for Donald to have known. To King Donald, the man simply appeared to be an out-of- control individual who was intent on attacking him, and that is why it was completely fair when Donald threw the man against the wall and then down the stairs. It was a terrible tragic misunderstanding.

Afterwards, King Donald, determined to not let a misunderstanding ruin his charitable work, proceeded on to the children's cancer treatment ward with his entourage. The treatment ward was divided into two large separate rooms: The Prince's Ward and The Princess's Ward. King Donald, while standing outside the The Princess's Ward, instructed his security staff to stay outside while he went in and visited with the children. Wanting it to be a friendly visit, he was afraid the security staff uniforms might frighten the poor children. He was looking to have some quality private time with the poor little sick girls in order to reassure them that regardless of the outcome of their sickness, they should always remember that their great King Donald truly loved them and that he would always be right there behind them. Donald wisely understood the phrase "the children are the future" in much the same way that so many popular musicians understood it. I truly believe our king understands how to influence young children better than anyone else in the kingdom.

Unfortunately, just as he had begun to open the door to the ward, Mrs. Khrump showed up suddenly, surprising everyone there. She shouted "NO" at the top of her voice and then yanked the king's hand hard from the door handle. Something was obviously very wrong with her, because she was shaking terribly and seemed to be nearly out of her mind with panic. Over the next few moments she selfishly insisted to the crowd that the two of them needed to leave immediately because they had a previous engagement that they had forgotten about and were already late for.

At that point, she whisked him away to a waiting car and just like that they were gone. It was a terrible tragedy that those poor little girls had to miss out on the opportunity of spending some private time with our wonderful king that day. However, I am confident that one day he'll find his way back there and make up for it.

I'll admit to my readers that Mrs. Khrump's controlling behavior toward our king that day did somewhat "rub me the wrong way," as it would any other male in touch with his masculine side. It was because of that behavior that I felt a need to show our great king that I and all other masculine males in our kingdom were firmly behind him, so I put together a small secret petition to suggest to him that perhaps next time he doesn't need to be so quick to do what she asks of him. I wanted our king to know that we had his back in the same way that we always felt that he had ours. It just didn't seem right for her to be treating him that way, considering that just the previous day he had issued his long-overdue executive decree that protected men from a similar kind of aggressive behavior. On the other hand, knowing our king the way I do, I'm sure that once they arrived back home to the palace that night, he most likely gave her a talking-to about her unacceptable behavior, and I'm sure she was straightened right out. That being said, if it had been me in his position, I would have made sure that she'd have been wearing dark sunglasses for a few days, if you know what I mean.

Day Twenty-Five

The giant stage platform outside the enormous coal processing facility in Kochlahoma City was decorated with giant flags and banners in our great kingdoms colors of blue, white, and red. The surrounding stadium seats were filled nearly to capacity with local coal industry workers along with their families and friends. As I looked around, I saw quite a few people sitting there who were hooked up to portable oxygen tanks. Others in the crowd seemed to be too thin and had oddly discolored skin, which most likely indicated years and years of terrible illness and disease.

That crowd had certainly suffered quite a bit and through multiple generations, and yet there they were, refusing to move away. Why? I believe it's because they've always been some of our toughest hard-core kingdom citizens.

King Donald was holding the rally there that day in order to make an incredibly important announcement concerning our kingdom's clean air and water. My network, Fix News, was the only news network being allowed to cover the event, and it felt pretty good to be trusted by our king.

The sun was shining high in the sky on that beautiful afternoon when suddenly one of the processing facility doors swung violently open and slammed against the side of the building. King Donald, standing there in the doorway, walked out into the sun, up the steps to the platform, and quickly over to the podium. After a few minutes of graciously accepting the applause from the crowd, our charismatic King Donald began his speech. It was a bit long, but it was amazing, so I've included most of it here.

"Coal! Oil! Always such exciting words! Always such exciting industries! Your amazing and magical 'Man Who Lives in the Clouds' gave us these gifts from the earth for a reason!" King Donald's eyes were burning red with passion! "He gave us these gifts to utilize! To make our lives better! What is there to not understand?"

The crowd erupted in shouting and applause. Honestly, even I, a perfect professional veteran newsman, found myself being swept up in our king's passion, and even found myself silently responding to his questions the way a man in church reacts to a preacher passionately speaking of "The Man in the Clouds" while pounding on his pulpit.

"Look at you people! Still living and working here even after generations of death and disease from coal dust and disgusting water made poisonous by runoff from the mine. You're all used to being told you're stupid, or you're saps, or maybe that you're suckers! I know the truth, though, and the truth is that you're all hard-core, and I respect that. When the going got tough, did you move your family away and maybe get an education in some other field because your industry was dying? Hell no, you didn't! You're hard-core, and you stuck it out."

"Everybody in our kingdom blames you people and your industries here for all the environmental pollution. I hear this all the time. Well, today, I have huge news about our environmental pollution, and you're going to be shocked and amazed when you hear it. This is big news, very big news, and you people here will be the first ones to hear it. As your beloved king, I have access to information, lots and lots of information, and let me tell you, when you hear this, it is going to rock your world, so hold on to your hats."

"Here it is, and it's incredible. I have just found out that our despised previous king, King Chezvic Dandyfoyl, along with his administrative officials, conspired for years to keep you from knowing the truth about air and water pollution. It hurt me when I found out the truth, because I always trusted the guy. I liked the guy, and I supported him in so many ways, but now I feel the same way that all of you are going to feel in a few moments when you hear it. Well, here it is folks, in all its horror."

"This is a story of environmental terrorism. The far far eastern kingdoms of our world have been storing their air and water pollution deep in the ground for years! Many many years, and guess what? Your King Dandyfoyl knew about it. He knew about it for years and years and he did nothing. He allowed it. He knew, and he allowed them to do it. It's a scandal, that's what it is. He failed you. He failed all of you because every bit of that pollution traveled underground to our kingdom, came up through cracks in the earth, and polluted all our air and water. I'm no rocket scientist, so I can't really tell you the nuts and bolts about how it happened, but believe me, it happened.

"King Dandyfoyl and his administration failed our kingdom by allowing environmental terrorism to become widespread here. They had a responsibility to protect you, but they failed. I, however, will protect you. I will protect you and your families and our environment, and I will start today. My new executive decree will provide for military action if any of the far far eastern kingdoms do not stop these horrific environmental terrorist acts against our kingdom. This will be the first decree of many, and if they do not comply, I am prepared to have our military launch a preemptive strike.

"Today is going to be remembered as the day our kingdom achieved freedom from the foreign environmental terrorists. The day that unjust domestic environmental regulations that were not working, and were in fact destroying our kingdom's corporations, were finally done away with. The day that we began to make our kingdom great again. The coal and oil industries were never the problem. They were simply the victims of misidentification. Finally, they can be allowed to do what they do best: serve the people. With the unjust environmental regulations that have been strangling our industries finally done away with, our industries will be able to thrive! Their lower business costs will mean higher profits, which in turn might mean the trickling down of some of those profits to you, the great people of our great kingdom!

"We do need to be aware that there may be a period of environmental conditions adjustment during which time the pollution levels may rise to higher levels before falling to the final true lower levels. If this occurs, please be assured, it will only be temporary, and I and my administration will be prepared. My former business associates have told me they have arranged to have solutions ready just in case such a temporary event occurs.

"Regardless of whether you are rich or poor, there will be solutions ready and available for every citizen. In the same way there are bottled water products for every taste and lifestyle, there will be safe compressed pure delicious air and air filtration devices for every citizen. I will even have my very own extensive brand of products available for purchase, but because I feel it would be unfair for me to mention my full product line here today, I'll just say that when you go online, you should look for 'Khrump Air, It's All There.'

"Our beloved kingdom will be the world's frontrunner in a new landscape of golden opportunities! Think about this. Years ago, everyone said you couldn't possibly make money from selling plain bottled water because of the availability of tap water in everyone's home. It was understood that only the wealthiest citizens would be willing to buy bottled water, and in that instance, it would have to be exotic water, perhaps glacial melt water or some such thing. Oh, but look at the world now! How many of you in the stadium are holding bottles of plain water? See? The bottled water industry has become a multi-billion-dollar industry!

"Purified air could become the next such industry! Our kingdom could possibly have the opportunity to become the world leader in the personal purified air industry! Who here loves pure mountain air? We all do. It's cool, it's crisp, and it's refreshing. Imagine breathing in that beautiful mountain air while in the comfort of your own home, or while you're zipping down the road in your new exclusive Mercedes sedan. The thought of it is beautiful, just beautiful."

King Donald's face seemed to be glowing and almost angelic in some ways. Perhaps it was "The Man in the Clouds" speaking through him.

"Delicious compressed brand-name quality air. Who

wouldn't want that? We all would. I know I would. Minty scented air, chocolate mousse scented air, wet air, dry air, perfumed air, you name it, whatever you want, you can have, because your kingdom's biggest corporations will be running the show and they will be running it for you. You want an air filtration mask with a scent that reminds you of a walk on the beach while you walk your dog in your city? You got it. A whole house system? You got it. You own the show, so let's get this show on the road folks. Your corporations love you, I love you, and I promise you now, you will all get exactly what you want. I am your beloved King Donald and, because I care about you so much, I promise you that you will all get exactly what you deserve."

Day Thirty-One

After the most productive first thirty days of any new king's reign in our entire kingdom's history, I somewhat expected day thirty-one to be a day of rest for King Donald. I was wrong. It turned out instead to be a symbolic day where our king showed us that regardless of one's class affiliation, all citizens will be afforded equal attention and protections under the laws of our land.

The well-known and occasionally sensationalistic news network The Virtual Enquirer broadcast a story about union laborers in an industry that most of us never think about. The evening's in-depth interview was with the local representatives of the Kingdom's Sex Workers Union. The representatives claimed there were concerns being raised from their local union members about the possibility that their new king might possibly put restrictions on the union workers' abilities to make a decent living because of the new king's close relationships with many of the heads of various houses of worship within the kingdom.

Upon being made aware of this, King Donald, always willing to listen to all citizens concerns, immediately invited the union's head representative, Bunny Soxalot, and her associates, Debi and Dona Yumyum, the famous twin performers, to a closed- door meeting at the central palace. In the spirit of creating a less intimidating experience for the representatives first visit to the central palace, King Donald showed up to the conference room wearing his favorite white silk robe and rainbow flip-flops. He was overheard saying, just before the conference room door closed for the meeting, that he had complete confidence that within just a few hours, they would have an agreement completely banged out that would absolutely guarantee the union workers a permanent right to work in the kingdom.

King Donald, a master negotiator, knew with confidence that he could craft an agreement that would be sure to satisfy everyone. From outside the room, it was clear that an intense, energetic debate was going on inside the room, due to all the shouting and name-calling that could be heard filtering out through the surrounding walls. Later, after just a few hours of what seemed like perhaps the most passionate negotiations to have ever taken place within the palace walls, an agreement/guarantee was finally reached. To celebrate, King Donald phoned out to the main palace kitchen and ordered some light snacks along with a few bottles of celebratory champagne to be brought to the conference room.

Interestingly, the air conditioning vents of the conference room seemed to have malfunctioned during the intense negotiations, which resulted in the conference room becoming unbearably hot. Because of this, the kitchen staff had to also bring along a large stack of towels and an industrial size box of wetnaps to aid in the sweaty clean-up.

Afterwards, as his guests were leaving, King Donald, always wanting to encourage citizen interest in the kingdom's governmental processes, graciously offered all three of the union representatives the opportunity to return to the palace once each week in order to be updated on any potential union-related legislation.

Day Thirty-Four

Day thirty-four was a proud, patriotic day. Around twelve noon, the main palace issued a surprise press release to all media networks. It was revealed that on the previous night, in a southwestern border town, a small group of brave kingdom citizens had come together as one, and even though most of them had had no formal military training, they were still able to successfully defend our kingdom against a large group of expertly trained invaders. Our great kingdom had come under vicious attack from "brownie" narcotics dealers attempting to cross through the border fence that we share with the Kingdom of Metexaco.

The drug dealers were disguised as poor peasants and young children, who, while trying to untangle themselves from the barbed wire of the fencing, kept screaming and crying loudly about how they were supposedly being chased by some group of dangerous criminals. It was probably at least a little difficult to make out what they were saying because of that low-class accent they use when they try to speak our language, but still, regardless of what they were saying, anyone with half a brain would have known that it was a lie anyway. Some of them, particularly the smaller adults who were pretending to be children, were able to tear themselves free from the barbed wire, at which point they tried running away, and, from what we were told, some of them nearly made it.

Luckily for all of us in our precious kingdom, though, the heroic well-armed militia members were not going to be fooled that easily. They had been taught how to handle situations like that through their militia membership pamphlets, in particular about how all "brownie" cartel soldiers had been trained in deception and were absolute masters of disguise. Every militia member knew exactly what was going on. There may have been only eighteen militia members there that night, but they were well armed and they had the "Man Upstairs" on their side.

After only a few minutes, it was over, and all one hundred and twenty-six invaders were dead. Miraculously, not even one militia member was harmed, at least not by an invader. We were informed that the youngest militia member Scott Manleemn, the son of our kingdom's toughest and most famous sheriff, Joe Michael Manleemn, did however suffer a slightly sprained trigger finger because of the nature of semi-automatic weapons. He reported to the palace: "I couldn't fire fast enough. I tried to get all them invader drug 'brownies,' but my trigger finger froze up. I'll have to do some kind of special exercises so it don't happen next time. The taller ones were fast, but the smaller ones were really easy to pick off."

It brought a tear to my eye to think about such incredible heroism while I was writing this page. I'm sure his parents felt very proud having such a brave and patriotic son.

Day Thirty-Six

It was a day of terrible injustice! I considered it an act of treason when a news network in our kingdom gave fifteen minutes of air time to the head of an enemy kingdom during which it promoted an obviously fake news story that slandered our national heroes. My humble opinion was that the people in charge needed to be punished, and punished immediately!!

Two days after the attempted invasion of our country by "brownie" drug lords at the Metexaco border, the king of Metexaco, Suavince Foxx, was interviewed on the AVN Network evening news show *Hindsight 20/20*. During the interview, King Foxx claimed that while a tragedy had occurred at our shared border two nights before, it was a different sort of tragedy than the one that had been reported through our palace press release.

He told the show's host, "Our military police drug enforcement division had spent months hunting down and apprehending a large group of suspected criminals who we believed were high level drug cartel kingpins. This was possible because of a very brave group of informers who came from the border towns. These people had come forward a few months earlier and had assisted us with identifying the individual cartel members. Thanks to them, we have some of the very worst of the drug kingpins in custody right now awaiting trial. Unfortunately, somewhere along the line, it appears that the identities of the informants had become known to the cartel."

"A few nights ago, the cartel kingpins sent out enforcers to punish the informers and their families. As everyone knows, the cartel leaders believe in brutal punishment for anyone who dares to inform on its members. The enforcers were tracking these brave individuals and their families and had nearly caught up to them at the border. That's the point at which your mentally deficient morally bankrupt citizen insects with guns, who could have helped them, instead helped the cartel kingpins by doing what the enforcers had been sent out to do."

"Thanks to your idiot self proclaimed border guard bozos, we now have no one to testify against the cartel kingpins. Your idiots murdered one hundred twenty-six innocent people, many of them young children. Do you people even know that attempting to enter your country illegally is a civil offense and not a criminal one? My God, your government actually allows morally vacant inbred white desert circus monkeys access to firearms? You people really need to look into that."

That's right. He actually said that. The reporter didn't stop him or cut it out of the interview. He actually called our heroes "morally vacant inbred white desert circus monkeys." I was as outraged as every other good and decent citizen was that night. That interview should never have been allowed to air. I knew that there needed to be a prompt and proper response to set the record straight, so I immediately called our king and convinced him to sit for an interview on my show that would be broadcast live on Fix News the following night. It was a brilliant interview, and thankfully, it set the record straight. As straight as an arrow.

Day Thirty-Seven

I presented my Fix News interview with King Donald. Before the broadcast began, he and I went over some of the issues we were to cover. The interview was broken into two parts, the "brownie" invasion, and a man's right to peace. We both considered these topics to be two of our kingdom's most pressing issues. The following are transcribed excerpts from the broadcast.

Me: Good evening, King Donald, and thank you for coming to our humble studio. I'm sure you're as excited to be here as we are to have you.

KD: Phil, it is an absolute pleasure to be here. I know you have quite a sizable audience, and this will be a great way for me to reach them. It's not as big as the audience I usually get just about anywhere I give a speech, but it's still a nice-sized audience.

Me: Consider it yours, King Donald. Let's get right to it, shall we? I imagine there might be something you'd like to say to King Suavince of Metexaco concerning the claims he made the other night?

KD: Phil, King Suavince is a ridiculous man making ridiculous claims. If he had a clue about how to run his kingdom, this would never have happened. Instead of me being here with you making a rebuttal, he and I would be sharing a few drinks in his wonderful palace ballroom while beautiful young girls would be giving each of us a lap dance while at the same time, our wives would be busy preparing a feast for us in the palace kitchen. If it was my palace, they'd definitely be preparing a couple of huge thick-cut exclusive restaurant-quality Omaha steaks! Seeing as it would be his palace though, hey, who knows? For all I know, his wife might be wanting to make us tacos or something because I'm pretty sure that's their national food there. It's not too bad, if you like that stuff, but personally, I'd prefer a steak.

Me: Well, I can understand that.

KD: I'm sure you can. Now, getting back to that other thing. I know for a fact that we were nearly invaded a few nights ago because I have access to a lot of information. I also know that the people who attacked us that night were all adult members of the "brownies" drug cartel special forces. My sources told me they breed those people for height, and when they run out, they do special surgeries on other members to make them shorter. Don't ask me how they do it, because I'm no rocket scientist, but I've been told by very high-level sources that that's what they do. You can trust me on this. Our militia forces there that night performed proudly and are great heroes.

Me: I completely trust you, and I completely agree with you as well.

KD: I'm sure you do. Hey, how is that little hottie co-anchor of yours? Hanna something? She can give me a lap dance if she's not doing the news. I don't mind. Maybe something will come up and I can give her a memory to tell her grandkids about someday.

Me: Actually, she's at home today, King Donald, but I'm sure she would love the opportunity to show you her respect sometime.

KD: I'm sure she would. Tell her I promise I'll make it happen.

Believe me, she can trust me on that one. Hey, one of the judges I appointed the other day told me a joke. I think you'll like it. He said, "If the 'brownies' and the 'scarfheads' wanted all the protections our constitution gives to our citizens, then they should have had the good sense to have been born here." Funny funny man, that guy. That's one of my requirements to be appointed, you know. They have to be able to make me laugh. There's something else that I want to explain to your audience, Phil.

Me: I'm sure they're listening. We all appreciate your amazing wisdom and guidance.

KD: It's about the executive order I issued the other day. The one about stopping unfair treatment of men by aggressive women. Well, I was thinking about it and decided that it didn't go far enough, so I'm going to amend it. I'm going to add a clause that I'm calling the "barefoot and pregnant clause." It's to honor the traditional idea that a woman's place is in the home of a man who has decided to share his life with her, and, by doing so, has accepted the responsibility to guide her. The clause states that if a woman pesters a man, but not necessarily accuses him of assault, and they are in some form of relationship, perhaps she is his girlfriend or wife or perhaps his mistress, and, after a short investigation, she is found by a judge to be truly incapable of rational thought in regard to their relationship, the man is to be made legal custodian of the woman until such time as a court decides she is clearheaded again. I made this decision because I absolutely love all women, and I feel a need to protect them. It's not their fault they're all like that, it's just the way they were made by the "Man Upstairs." I'll bet the religious crackajacks will love that one, Phil. I love those people. I love them, and they love me too. Great people, great families. Really great-looking families, and great-looking kids too. Really great-looking kids. I love those gorgeous kids.

Me: There you have it, folks. The truth, the whole truth, and nothing but the king's truth. I'm sending a big thanks to the "Man Upstairs" for having the wisdom to send our great king to us, plus another big thanks to King Donald for having the courage to just be himself. Our kingdom is truly blessed.

Day Forty-Two

For forty-one days, the implementation of King Donald's much- needed multilayered plan for our kingdom had progressed smoothly. Then, on day forty-two, that progress ground to a halt, a cruel literal halt. Something ridiculous had happened: a protest march. When I heard about it, I was both disappointed and frustrated. How had our good kingdom come to this? What had happened to civility and respect for authority? The protest was ridiculous and yet still effective, because the marchers were able to stop traffic in and around the kingdom's capital. After they had created all sorts of delays for everyone there, they moved on to the central palace square.

The protesters, who I'm sure were at least 99% Dreamocrats, were there to protest the special campgrounds that had been built for the "brownies" and the "scarfheads" that, according to the protesters, were unfair and immoral. As everyone knows, that claim is grotesquely inaccurate. The camps were built for one reason only: to allow the most unpopular minorities in our kingdom to prove to us, the legitimate citizens, that they were serious about being good and appreciative and trustworthy citizens. What better reason could there be? By the way, as a testament to our king's well-thought-out planning, the camps were functioning smoothly and efficiently. So smoothly, in fact, that with both camps more than filled to capacity, additional plans were made to construct even more. That is, unless King Donald and his brilliant planners could come up with a way to relieve the camps overcrowding without building more. I had faith they'd come up with some sort of excellent solution, seeing as he and his planners were all very creative men.

Looking out from the palace windows and feeling empathy for the protesters who were obviously misinformed about the nature of the campgrounds, King Donald decided to do something right then and there to correct the misperception. He walked out through the main level palace double doors and made his way to the central platform in the center of the square. He announced to the crowd that he would be willing to take time out of his busy schedule that day as long as he could meet with the leaders of the march immediately to address any concerns or misgivings the marchers may have had concerning the special camps.

At that point, two young female college students, Donna White and Jessica Canwell, came out of the crowd, walked up the stairs, introduced themselves, and thanked him for the opportunity to speak with him. For ten minutes he listened patiently as the protest leaders clumsily explained, to both him and to the crowd, their concerns about the unfairness and cruelty of the camps. During their entire sermon, King Donald, showing grace and class, stood there respectfully and listened.

When they were done, he thanked them, turned, and addressed the crowd. First, he told them how surprised he was that such an enormous and well-organized protest march could have been accomplished without his security staff having known about it in advance. That alone, he told them, was truly amazing, and was something they should be very proud of. He then told them how much he appreciated and understood their concerns, and announced that he already had what he believed to be an excellent plan that, incredibly, he had been working on just moments before when he learned there were protesters marching through the streets.

He then outlined his plan to the crowd. It was a wonderful plan, an absolutely fair and wonderful plan. King Donald told the crowd how he would arrange to have special employment opportunity centers set up inside each camp where all the camp residents would be allowed to list their individual special work skills that they felt might be of use to the kingdom. The campground administrators would use the lists to identify the properly skilled camp residents who were suitable for specific job opportunities for public and private kingdom projects. Using this system, if a job opportunity was to come up, the camp resident with the needed skill would be notified by an administrator. If the camp resident accepted the job offer, he or she would be seen to be graciously showing their respect and affection for the kingdom through their selfless act of volunteering to perform excellent quality unpaid work. By doing this, the resident would receive the king's assurance of possible special consideration for them and their families, if, at some time in the future, they were to decide to apply for permanent kingdom residency.

As I said earlier, it was a fair and wonderful plan, and I'm sure my readers agree. Unfortunately, some of the protesters there that day didn't seem to think so. Some of the troublemakers in the crowd began to shout loudly, while some others started waving their signs around. King Donald calmly put up his hands and asked for just a moment more of their attention. When the crowd quieted down, he thanked them and turned to face the leaders of the march. He invited Miss White and Miss Canwell to the main palace for a surprise rewards banquet that had been specially prepared for them.

The young ladies seemed somewhat surprised and a little reluctant at first, but King Donald gently insisted they come because the event had already been arranged, and he had even invited their entire families to be part of the celebration. It was just one more example of the appreciation our king has for the independent-minded youth of our kingdom. Plus, what an incredible coincidence that the protest leaders who were there that day just happened to be the same citizens he was already planning to honor! It was almost as if the "Man Upstairs" had planned this day all along. I can only imagine what the young ladies were thinking. What an amazing day for our kingdom!

Day Forty-Five

Canadinia, the large island kingdom just off our northern shores, should have been named Lumberland instead. Up there, life is all about trees, snow, and more trees. While its citizens may not be the most intelligent citizens in our civilized world, there is something they really do understand better than anyone else: how to process trees. Their kingdom engineers, after years of trial and error, had successfully developed a super-modern, ultra-efficient automated system for cutting and processing trees into an enormous variety of building materials, with an emphasis on lumber specifically designed and sized for single-family homes. While this development has been wonderful for Canadinia, with its simple rural tastes, it has been devastating for other kingdoms such as our own. Their irresponsible decision to sell cheap lumber directly to the lower and middle-class members of our kingdom through a special permit has helped to create a boom in the building of terribly unattractive lower-priced single-family homes. In short, this boom has been destroying our precious kingdom's beautiful sense of style.

Luckily, after seeing this tragedy unfold for far too long, a group of concerned men, myself included, decided to petition King Donald for relief. On day forty-five of his rule, just a few days after receiving our petition, King Donald issued an executive order that thankfully put an end to it. The cheap importation of building materials specifically meant for the lesser classes was finally seen as the social poison that it has always been. It was an enormous moral victory. All wealthy individuals and corporations know how cruel it is to burden lesser-class individuals with the responsibilities of home ownership, especially when there are so many class-appropriate rental properties readily available for them.

It takes vision and an educated spirit to be able to understand a buildings placement in relation to the environment which will allow it to be pleasing to the eye. When the lesser classes build homes, they are nearly always an immediate eyesore. Oh, perhaps one-tenth of one percent will get lucky, but that's the same as making a cockroach walk through a maze hoping it will find its way to the exit. It's just cruel. They simply don't have the gifts to understand style. When they're allowed to express their lower-class tastes, our kingdom's high aesthetic standard is guaranteed to fall. Yes, we all know they mean well, yet the reality is that their non-educated tastes are reliably terrible. No one wants to say it, but style experts know it's true. Square box homes with small windows and multicolored plastic flower gardens with cheap store-bought seasonal lawn decorations do absolutely nothing to increase the beauty of our kingdom.

On day forty-five, finally, thankfully, it became a little more out of reach for the lesser classes to build their cheap and hideous ideas of style. Also contained within the executive order was a small amendment that would require all single-family home permit applicants to provide to the licensing board a single-family home community needs assessment. This was added as a way to ensure equal investment protection for all citizens, including hard- working apartment complex corporate owners to ensure every citizen would have a powerful voice in our communities. It was a wonderful day of fair treatment being ensured for all. It felt like another miracle from "The Man Upstairs."

Day Fifty

After forty-nine of the most exciting and productive days ever by a new king in the entire history of our kingdom, King Donald, on day fifty, decided that, rather than take a well deserved rest, he would instead use that day to create a new replacement healthcare system he named The Alternative Magic Health Plan, or as I and my friends like to call it, "MagicCare." King Donald met with his advisors before the sun had even come up that day, and by midmorning they had crafted a rock-solid first- class replacement plan. For too many years, our kingdom citizens had suffered under the previous King Dandyfoyl's terrible healthcare plan, the Affordable Health Systems Plan, or, as many of us liked to call it, "DandyCare." King Dandyfoyl's "DandyCare" was his own personal signature stain that he had forced every face of every citizen to be rubbed into.

While there were some who said that only a few simple changes were needed to improve the plan's fairness and efficiency, we all knew in our good citizens' hearts that those simple changes would never be enough to make us accept his "DandyCare." We all felt that "DandyCare," having been brought to life by such an evil obnoxious know-it-all, simply had to go. Being so much like a hideous poisonous thorny vine, his plan had wound itself around all aspects of helping to make all kingdom citizens healthy, and as such, it needed to be pulled out by the roots. All citizens knew that King Donald, being naturally good at heart, would be the perfect one to do it. Like us, he saw that only a complete and total destruction of "DandyCare" could bring about the health care system changes that were so badly needed. King Donald's "MagicCare" would not only be a vastly improved and much fairer citizen health plan, but it would also be a platform for exciting alternative health care treatments that had, for far too long, been misunderstood and often derided by the mainstream healthcare professionals. It was finally time to give holistic healthcare concepts their proper respect. For so many years, snobbish healthcare professionals kept far away from holistic therapies because of so-called "small to zero value" benefits based on mainstream empirical scientific analysis. That would all be in the past, though, because King Donald would open up the system to much-needed change. He believed that "empirically driven science" was more of a roadblock than a path to acceptance, so, with just a few strokes of his pen our king changed skepticism to instant acceptance.

Who really needed MRI's and CT scans and chemotherapy when we could have far less expensive methods and treatments that were just as effective? Personally, I had never heard of Hot Rock Therapy, but it certainly costs less than seeing a specialist for myalgia. Reiki is a wonderful method of healing ourselves, and again, much much less expensive than a visit to a specialist who might just want to cut you open and rip out some piece of you in order to pay for a new yacht he has his eye on. By opening up our healthcare system to all manner of alternative therapies and medications, our king not only immediately improved the future health of all kingdom citizens, he also reduced the overall cost for treatments, which in turn thankfully drastically reduced the unholy burden of forced excessive health taxes that had been destroying our large beloved corporations. It was an amazing day for everyone. That is what winning looks like.

For the healthcare transition team, King Donald smartly installed top CEO's and CFO's from Big Tobacco, in particular Phil Morse, executive extraordinaire. By choosing such powerful individuals, he showed everyone he was truly serious about change. King Donald understood there was the small possibility that some citizens might be skeptical of the merits of the new system. In the unlikely scenario those citizens were to get together with a rogue scientist from the scientific community and then publicly express skepticism about our new health care system, Morse and his team would be there to deal with them. Big Tobacco had a long history of dealing with skeptics, mainly due to the fact that their excellent products had been unfairly maligned in the public opinion arena for so many years. Their industry had been a scapegoat for so long; an innocent victim of so many unproven accusations. For me, Big Tobacco had always been a big part of my life, as well as the lives of my friends. I remember so many good years of being able to share a good smoke with my friends while at work, as well as occasionally enjoying a good five-dollar cigar during lunch. That was before the unfair over-reaching smoking regulations were passed of course. Sometimes, I've asked myself, how did tobacco go from being a sacred part of our indigenous Indians' spiritual ceremonies to being a poisonous cancer on our pop culture landscape? Tobacco never had any connection to illness or death. We, the faithful church goers, all know that those sorts of things are decided by "The Man Upstairs." Morse and his associates had my complete and total confidence. I knew that if some citizens we to have doubt as to the effectiveness of holistic medicines, Morse and his crew would know how to take care of it.

Day Fifty-Five

It was a very sad day for King Donald. He was a victim yet again when his beloved Khrump family compound was broken into a second time. Luckily, there was no one there at the time due to the living quarters of the compound having been closed up since around the time of King Donald's coronation. Only the family zoo area of the compound was still active, because of the many caretakers and veterinarian specialists who needed to visit the zoo daily to care for the large number of exotic animals. A small but very valuable handful of King Donald's own personal items had been taken from his childhood bedroom. His adoptive father Fritz Khrump always kept his son's bedroom exactly as it had been on that first day when he had been welcomed into the Khrump family. Of the items that had been taken, one item in particular stood out from the rest: a large polished-mirror-finish twenty-four-karat solid-gold plaque with the inscription "My Favorite Possession." The plaque had always hung like a toddler's mobile toy above King Donald's first small bed. The thief showed his callous insensitivity by the note that was left on the bed which read "jajajajaja."

After many hours of research, King Donald's linguistic and security experts were finally able to decode the message. It was decided that the thief must have been a foreigner due to the fact that in some "brownie" languages, the message would have read "hahahahaha." King Donald, being a man of quick thinking and fast action, immediately established a tip hotline to his palace security staff for citizens to call if they thought they might have information that would assist in the investigation. He and his security experts also announced that the tip line could be used by citizens to file complaints if they too felt that they had been victims of immigrant crime.

Day Fifty-Nine

Nine days after our king replaced "DandyCare" with his brilliant "MagicCare," the transition was complete, and our kingdom's citizens were beginning to enjoy the benefits of the most open-minded modern health care system ever. Unfortunately, as is always the case, there were a few citizens who decided they didn't want change, even if it was for the better. One of those citizens, a woman from the lower classes, decided to launch her own illegal personal protest event. Somehow, she managed to sneak past the security guards into the palace, and eventually she found her way to the main dining hall. From what I've been told, she didn't appear to be a "brownie" or a "scarfhead," but she may as well have been because of the complete and total lack of manners and civility she displayed while being apprehended. A card-carrying Dreamocrat, I'm sure.

Dinner was being served to King Donald and some of his closest friends and staff when she barged into the dining hall through a service door, stopped, and called across the room to King Donald. She demanded to speak with him. Of course, everyone thought it was a joke, but then she became hysterical and wouldn't stop yelling and screaming, so the security guards finally grabbed her and tackled her to the ground. King Donald and his guests were confused for a moment, but the moment passed, and everyone went back to enjoying their dinner.

One of the palace guards who was there on duty, a friend of mine, filled me in with the details about what happened. He told me that while they were walking her down to the holding cell in the basement of the palace, she wouldn't shut up and kept going on and on about all her problems. She claimed she was working two jobs and at the same time was also going to school to become a nurse when her three-year-old son had become sick. He was diagnosed with leukemia and was scheduled for a stem cell transplant when she had received notification from her health insurer that her son's treatment would be changing. In place of the stem cell transplant procedure, he would instead be receiving a special price reduction coupon booklet each week that would be good for fifty percent discounts on: one pound of beansprouts, six green tea bags, one pint of honey, one quart of cactus juice, and a one-hour hot rock therapy session at "We Do the Hot Rocks Thing." She said that while that might be fine for some people who might not know any better, she would prefer that her son receive the treatment that was already decided on because it seemed to her to be a better course.

I asked him if she was pretty and if she had a nice body, and he told me she would have been a lot prettier if her eyes hadn't been so swollen and red from crying so much. He said they put her in the cell for a little while until she calmed down, and then they sent her home. I think she was very lucky to have gotten off so easily. I'm sure if King Donald had known exactly what she had done at that time, she would have received a much more appropriate punishment. Behavior like hers should never be tolerated. I find it truly discouraging when people behave in such a spoiled way, as if the world only revolves around them. Nine days earlier, our great king and his advisers spent nearly an entire day working on the incredibly complex issue of healthcare for all the kingdom's citizens, and, after coming up with an amazingly holistically inclusive and perfectly fair health plan, while at the same time saving the better members of our kingdom an enormous amount of money, that woman actually thought it was socially acceptable to behave in such an unappreciative fashion.

Being a faithful believer in our "Man in the Clouds" and his master plan, I am absolutely certain there must have been a reason for her and her son to have been going through such a period of terrible suffering. She must have done something despicable during her lifetime to have had our "Man Upstairs" feel the need to make her and her son suffer in that way. The "Man Upstairs" has always been known for his fairness, so if you know someone who is suffering, you can bet it is of their own doing.

It's tiring to hear the "have-nots" complain about the "haves." King Donald and I have talked about this many times before. Men like King Donald and I are the "haves" because we are better, stronger, more intelligent, and more beautiful. We have beautiful children. We have beautiful wives and mistresses. We have more of everything because we deserve more. We own the largest corporations. We buy and sell our company stocks as if it's a game, because we can. It's a privilege that we deserve. We choose to give ourselves huge bonuses instead of our hard- working lesser-class employees, because it would do them no good anyway. They would only blow it on drugs or alcohol or gambling.

King Donald's popularity among the lesser classes is an inspiration to the members of the upper one percent. His election success showed us that it is time to accept who we are. There is no longer a need to pretend to be the kind of people we're not. We no longer have to feel shame for who we are, or how we treat the less fortunate. He showed us it's okay to flaunt power and privilege. Kingdom citizens of all classes, in particular the least educated, finally recognize the absolute brilliance of us, the top one percent, and will now trust us completely. We're finally able to rip off our damning ethics shackles and officially redefine corruption in every sense of the word!

Day Sixty-Two

Ever since King Donald's coronation day, I've woken up with a big smile on my face and thought to myself, "What a wonderful day! Another wonderful day in paradise!" Day sixty-two was no different. After thanking "The Man Upstairs" for my vast and good fortune, I began to feel a powerful need, a need to show my kingdom pride. I felt a need to express to my friends and neighbors and my multitude of fans how much I loved my life. I thought, "What could possibly be the best way for me to show this while at the same time allow all other kingdom folks to show their own joy as well?" The answer came to me in a flash. A rally. A fantastic and incredible over-the-top college-football-style rally.

I grabbed my phone and immediately contacted my Fix News colleague and occasional co-host Lewis Dobson and explained my idea, along with the suggestion that perhaps we could hold the event that very evening. I explained how I thought we could celebrate the amazing changes King Donald had already accomplished, and then lay out the exciting new changes that were planned for the very near future. Lewis thought it was a fantastic idea, so we contacted King Donald to ask if he might be interested in being the Master of Ceremonies. King Donald immediately said yes and even suggested a way to show the kingdom his absolute commitment to real social change by inviting a father and son representative pair from one of the special campgrounds to share in the celebration. He would personally stop by the "scarfhead" campground and pick out what he considered a representative vacationing pair.

Both the "brownie" and the "scarfhead" campgrounds were operating at peak efficiency, and yet both were still having occasional issues with campers resisting the never mandatory always voluntary work program. King Donald felt it was a good time to symbolically show both sides just how united we all were as a people.

Being a true organizer and always looking for a challenge, King Donald also insisted on being personally involved in all preparations for the event, and, with his help, every detail was taken care of in only a few hours.

People began arriving at the square around one o'clock in the afternoon, and by seven o'clock in the evening, it was showtime. An enormous crowd filled the central palace meeting square, with the king's most passionate fans crowding toward the main stage that had been set up closest to the palace doors. The passion coming from the crowd that night was truly electrifying. The whole place had a wonderful exciting carnival-like atmosphere, complete with five-dollar games of chance, three open barbecue pits, and the longest free open bar counter in the whole kingdom, which snaked around the entire length of the meeting square. It promised to be a memorable evening, and it certainly was.

Thad Nouget, King Donald's favorite band, went onstage at seven o'clock sharp that night, and performed heroically for almost two hours before taking a break. The lead singer for Thad Nougat, F. N. Littldich, is a trusted and longtime friend of King Donald. They enjoy hunting together a few weekends each year, and make no secret of the fact that they like the game they find in the wooded areas around the northern ethnic campgrounds the best. Personally, I'm not much of a fan of Thad Nouget. It always seemed to me that their music was made specifically for the brain-dead lower classes, although I do admit I've heard rumors that there are some well-educated scholars who enjoy the band as well.

At nine o'clock sharp, just as the band finished up their crowd favorite, "Snot's Running Down My Face," F. N. Littldich asked for the crowd's attention and then welcomed

King Donald out onto the stage. The crowd went absolutely ballistic! It seemed as if King Donald was more of a rock star than F. N. Littldich!

King Donald addressed the crowd. "Are you having a good time?" he yelled out to them. The crowd went absolutely wild. He asked them again, "Are you having a good time?" and that time the crowd screamed back with a deafening "YES!" The noise level was out of this world! "Good!" he yelled back again, and then left the stage.

A few moments later, Lewis Dobson, my Fix News colleague, came out on the stage. Nearly everyone in the crowd knew Lewis from his Fix News Hour special report segments that tended to concentrate on the ethnic problems plaguing our kingdom. He yelled to the crowd, "Do you want to see some fair and balanced treatment?" The crowd roared! He yelled back to the crowd, "Me too!" Lewis turned and looked to the back of the stage and said, "Let's bring them out to meet my friends!"

A "scarfhead" man and his young son were shuttled out from the back of the stage and brought up to the front. They stood very close to each other and were right next to Lewis. Lewis asked them, "How do you like our kingdom?"

The man responded, "I like it very much. I've lived here for twenty years."

Lewis asked him, "Do you think you belong here?" to which the man said, "I like to think so."

Lewis then said, "You take our jobs and our women and the very air we breathe!" The little boy was shaking. The man said nothing. Lewis said, "Tell me what you think." Again the man said nothing. Lewis then said it again, but much louder: "Tell me what you think!" The man responded "I'm sorry, I do not think what you said is right." Lewis then screamed at the man, "I don't think it's right, either!" and then pushed the man off the stage into the screaming crowd. I'm sure they practiced it many times to get it just right.

The small "scarfhead" child then received the shock of his life when King Donald leaped out from the shadows at the back of the stage and landed right on top of him. I realized that King Donald kept himself in good shape, but I had no idea he was such a talented acrobat. I could barely keep myself from laughing at the frightened look on the child's face. As the crowd screamed and crowded around the man on the ground in front of the stage, King Donald savagely bit the child in the groin at least a dozen times right through his denim jeans. That was one "scarfhead" who wasn't going to be adding to our "scarfhead" campground population too soon. I'm just kidding, of course. Anyone with half a brain knows it was all just a show for the crowd. King Donald, Mr. TV, just hamming it up for his fans.

Earlier, right before the gates opened, King Donald told all of us there, "Let's give them what they want, folks. Let's give them an amazing show. Let's show them who and what we really are," and The Ultimate Showman King Donald did exactly that. Sure, the next day the Dreamocrats tried to claim the attacks were real, but that just shows how the brain of a Dreamocrat tends to function. Any agitation at all and they just shut down mentally and lose their ability to reason. The truth was, even though Lewis and I got swept up in the festival atmosphere and completely forgot about reading our speeches, King Donald saved the day by putting on a masterful performance.

Day Sixty-Six

Two terrible events occurred. First, the Khrump family compound was broken into yet again. Thankfully, this time, the thieves kept their activities to the family zoo building supplies area. After I heard about it, I kept thinking, why on earth would someone steal building supplies from the Khrump compound when they could steal them much more easily from any of the home improvement retail stores? The list of stolen items included fence and cage building materials, cement, and all sorts of power tools. It made no sense, but then again, no one ever said our thieves were the brightest individuals in our kingdom. My guess is that a group of "brownies" or "scarfheads" from one of the vacation campgrounds did it. Unfortunately, while surveillance cameras had been installed in the family compound living areas after the last break-in, no one at the time thought it was necessary to install cameras in the building supplies area. By the end of the day the thieves had not yet been arrested, but I had total confidence they soon would be. Kingdom Security Services was finally taking the break-ins very seriously because they realized the Khrump Compound would be a Kingdom Heritage Site one day.

The second terrible event of the day was when poor Kandy Ann Conroy, King Donald's personal food taster and favorite palace gofer, stopped breathing and fell down unconscious after sampling the king's typical evening dessert dish of chocolate-covered dried apricots and prunes. While the details are still unclear, it appears as if she may have ingested some sort of mild neurotoxin, or more likely may have had an allergic reaction to something in his food which inhibited her ability to breathe. She was resuscitated after nearly three minutes, and although everyone expected her to have at least a small amount of brain damage, I was told that because there was no noticeable difference in her behavior or personality, she was instructed to immediately go back to work.

Most people, outside of palace administration officials, are not familiar with Kandy because she tends to stay in the background most of the time. Before he was elected, she was one of King Donald's biggest fans, and had a definite "groupie" mentality. King Donald and his staff like her and have always found her to be an entertaining employee because, in the course of her work day, whenever Kandy is feeling agitated or upset for some reason, she starts having a very funny and very loud conversation with herself. This has never been a problem, because she's always managed to finish whatever tasks she's been assigned. With such personality quirks, though, King Donald has always had to be sure to keep her away from the palace press corps. You can just imagine what kind of nutty craziness she could concoct if she was ever given just two minutes with a reporter when she happened to be in one of her moods.

Once, during a palace cocktail party, after we both had a few too many drinks, she confided in me that when she was a small child, she had an unusual habit of hiding in the family bathroom closet. While in there, she would hit herself in the head with a plastic hammer from her little brother's toy tool box, while at the same time stuff pinto beans up her nose. I told her it was a good thing the hammer was plastic, or she could have done a lot more damage than she did. She then told me she was pregnant and was worried about how she was going to tell the father who happened to be married to someone else. Seeing as I wasn't a psychiatrist, that was my cue to leave. I'll tell you this though, she had one heck of an absolutely gorgeous curvy body, and I can certainly see why the father, whoever he was, did what he did. I'm also pretty sure she was into me that night, but the pregnancy thing turned me off like an ice-cold shower.

Near the end of the day, Cal Jhimly, head of Kingdom Security Services, learned of the potential food poisoning event and considered opening an investigation. King Donald, however, informed him that he had been reading extensively about allergic reactions and assured Jhimly that the event was most likely an accident, and the best decision would be to ignore it and not waste kingdom resources on something so trivial.

Day Seventy

It was a sad day for our king. Pollyryann, his favorite gelding, had to be put down after trying to attack his master. It was a terrible tragedy because up until that day, King Donald had always been able to rely on Pollyryann to do exactly as he was told. He was a very beautiful horse with a fabulous mane, and yet, unfortunately, after what he did in the stable that day, King Donald could not allow him to live.

Three months prior, just before his coronation, King Donald had chosen Pollyryann as his personal steed from the palace stables. He was exactly what the king was looking for, because Pollyryann did not have a mind of his own. Yes, there may be some who would have found that to be a weakness, but King Donald, with his superior judgement, found that trait to be Pollyryann's most valuable asset. His weak and puttylike mind made it possible for King Donald to bend Pollyryann to his will and get him to perform with an almost robot-like precision. When the two of them rode together they seemed like a perfect match made by "The Man in the Clouds" and yet, on day seventy, after months of loyal obedience, inexplicably, Pollyryann changed.

King Donald was in the palace stables getting Pollyryann ready to go riding that day, when a group of reporters from Fix News stopped by and asked if they could take a few photos of him with his horse. The network was airing an important special report that night titled "What's the king up to today?" They were there hoping for a few candid heroic-type shots of him on his favorite steed. Pollyryann had already been saddled up and was ready to go, so King Donald climbed on top and put him through a few basic types of poses that everyone likes to see. Afterwards, deciding to ham it up for the photographers, he began to put Pollyryann through some more complicated maneuvers. It was then that it happened. In an instant, Pollyryann seemed to have somehow grown an independent mind. He seemed to have decided that he had had enough of doing what his master desired. As everyone knows, that sort of selfish independent thinking has no place in our king's stables or even in his administration.

Pollyryann stopped midway through one of the more complicated maneuvers and bucked King Donald right off. Then, as our king tried to sit up, Pollyryann lunged at him and repeatedly tried to bite him. Luckily, King Donald was able to roll over to the side wall of the stable and grab the shotgun he always kept mounted on the wall. He yelled at Pollyryann to calm down and do as he was told, but he wouldn't listen. He reared up, came down and charged hard at King Donald, who stepped to the side and shot him in the neck six times. It was a terrible tragedy, but Pollyryann really didn't give King Donald much of a choice.

King Donald told me later, "It was almost as if Pollyryann

had forgotten his place in the world, and had begun to think of us as equals."

Indeed, it was a sad day, and I'm sure King Donald will always miss him and forever keep him in his heart. Luckily, there were many other geldings in the palace stables who had been waiting for just such a chance to impress their king with their love and loyalty, as well as their submissiveness. Two in particular stood out from the rest, Rokkid and Skottibee. Our king had used them in the past during the few rare occasions when Pollyryann had been under the weather. Rokkid was a good-looking horse with a bit of a wild streak in him, and yet at the same time, he always knew how to be subservient around King Donald. Skottibee, while not a very good-looking horse, had no wild streak at all. With King Donald, he could be so submissive and weak-minded that his behavior bordered on sniveling. He never would have been my choice, but King Donald did really enjoy Skottibee's company. I've been told that when King Donald entered his stall, Skottibee would roll over in the straw wanting to have his belly rubbed as if he was a puppy.

Having such a huge heart, King Donald loved them both, as well as all the other horses, and yet, none could ever compare to Sarahpea, He told me about her once during an interview. She was a beautiful mare he owned a long time ago that he kept up at the Khrump Compound family stables. He told me she was an amazing beauty from her long perfect legs and tail all the way up to her gorgeous chestnut mane and perfect teeth. Unfortunately, he told me, she was also dumb as a stump. King Donald told me how she was never able to understand that when she drank from a water basin, her reflection in the water was herself and not another horse trying to take her water. Each time she'd see her reflection, she'd plunge her head into the water and start thrashing and biting. Because of that, she always had to be kept away from water basins when there wasn't someone there to keep an eye on her. Unfortunately, the day came when there was no one there and she found a water basin. She saw herself in the water and started biting at her reflection and kept it up until she drowned herself. It was a terrible waste, and he said he would have laughed about it if she hadn't been such a beautiful prize.

Day Seventy-Four

It was an excellent day for excellent news. King Donald announced to the kingdom that on day one hundred of his reign, there was to be an official festival ball to celebrate the successes of his first one hundred days. He also announced that, as a reward to Fix News Network for its acts of loyalty to his administration as well as its help in spreading proper official palace news, the festival ball would be held in the Fix News Network Campus Ballroom. The entire staff of Fix News, myself included, felt a surge of pride when he made the announcement. We were truly overjoyed to publicly receive King Donald's recognition. My network and I had done our very best to be instrumental in helping his administration's policies to be realized. By our "Khrumping" the news each day, as we at the network liked to call it, and by volunteering to be the eyes and ears of his administration, with our representatives spread throughout our great kingdom, we had been able to aid him in sorting friends from foes far quicker than anyone ever realized could be possible.

I was a bit surprised by the announcement of a fancy ball instead of a more informal celebration, seeing as King Donald tended to prefer rally-style parties, but, after some consideration, I decided that the idea for the "ball" was probably his wife's seeing as that's the sort of thing a woman would come up with. After some more consideration, I realized that a fancy dress ball, broadcast on the Fix Network of course, would be a wonderful way for all my lesser class fans to be able to share in the spotlight.

Another excellent piece of news was that the vacation camps were beginning to show the most important sign of efficiency: they had managed to squeeze out a small but decent profit! Even better was that it was far earlier than King Donald or any of his advisors had projected. It may have been due in part to a strategy of doubling up the occupancy rate of each bungalow, as well as the auditing of meal portions, which was of course done to ensure there was no waste. It's amazing how just a few smart changes in feeding and housing policies had allowed for such an early profit, even with new campers continuing to arrive daily. There were, in fact, so many new campers coming in each day that King Donald decided to begin a trial run of his repatriation program. The program permitted a few camper families to leave the camps in order to spend some quality time back in their native kingdoms. Luckily for the palace staff and their associates, every one of the campers who had chosen to leave had also given their permission to allow their children to stay in the kingdom to be placed, at the king's discretion, in the appropriate palace staff offices and associate households for specific apprenticeship training. Those were some lucky kids! It was a win-win for everyone.

For security purposes, very few people were aware of the trial run at the time. King Donald and his advisors felt that if more people knew about the trial run, more may have wanted to participate, and King Donald wanted to iron out the details before the full repatriation program was underway. Results of the program were so good by the end of the day that King Donald decided the official announcement of the full program would come during his one hundredth day celebration, just a little more than three weeks away.

Day Seventy-Eight

Today, one of my sources, a guard over at the palace, told me how King Donald's wife Ninatina came walking into the inner palace courtyard looking very angry. He told me she walked up to him and demanded to see King Donald immediately. I asked him what she was wearing, because we all know there's nothing hotter than a gorgeous woman dressed up and pissed off, but he told me she was dressed normally and didn't seem to be wearing any makeup. Well, that completely let me down. I ask myself sometimes how women can ever expect to keep a hold on great men like King Donald or myself if they don't "work it."

Anyway, she suddenly started explaining to him that after touring the kingdom's northern textile factories, she stopped by one of the vacation camps to see how they operated. She told him that something seemed wrong or out of place because she had been told they were filled to capacity, and yet when she entered some of the dormitory buildings, they were empty except for some large piles of luggage. Obviously, as anyone could have guessed, the abandoned luggage was due to the high volume of belongings that some campers must have had. When they left, they were unable to take all of it with them, and were arranging for their remaining luggage to be shipped to them later. My source, however, seeing how agitated and angry she was, decided that, rather than point out the obvious to her, it was easier to just show her to the conference room where King Donald was having his lunch.

He told me she went in, closed the door, and was in there for about twenty minutes. Afterwards, when she came out, he said she seemed a little confused. She walked across the courtyard, stopped right in front of him, stood there for at least five seconds, and, without saying a word, turned and walked away.

Later in the evening, when I met with King Donald to go over a few of the details about the upcoming ball at Fix News, I remembered what the guard had told me, so I asked King Donald if he could tell me what they had talked about. He told me that after first telling her to calm down, he explained what was going on at the camps with the trial run of the new repatriation program. He then kindly offered that it would be okay for her to look through the campers' luggage and, if she saw something she liked, it would be okay for her to keep it. He assured her that the campers wouldn't mind a bit, and would in fact be very flattered if she was to take something of theirs home with her. Afterwards, he explained to her how he was having a very important meeting with a group of union representatives shortly, so it would be better if they talked about it later when he arrived home that evening.

Personally, I believe my source may have slightly misunderstood the situation. I know women pretty well, and I think that after having not seen her husband for a week, most of her urgency to see him probably had a lot more to do with her physical needs than anything related to any camper's luggage, if you know what I mean.

Day Eighty-Two

A huge day! Early in the day, the AVN Network had its license to operate suspended because of its failure to act in the public interest. Finally! King Donald's administration took this bold and very appropriate move just moments after the AVN finished a broadcast interview with Suavince Foxx, the King of Metexaco. In the interview, Foxx claimed to have heard rumors that a repatriation program had begun at one of our campgrounds, and yet, Foxx claimed, there had been no sign of any increased border activity at or near the Metexaco border processing centers. Fox further insulted our king and kingdom by demanding to be told where those people were, because he had also heard rumors that the people had perhaps been moved to jails and were being held illegally against their will. When informed about Foxx's accusations, King Donald, rightfully angry, immediately contacted Fix News to arrange for a taped response which would be broadcast that evening on the Fix Network Evening News. In his video response, King Donald looked fantastic, wearing his twenty- four-karat solid-gold crown, flowing red crushed-velvet cape, and his famous trademarked super-long, super-wide red power tie.

The video began with King Donald pointing out that King Foxx's inaccuracies were obviously the unfortunate effect of having poor-quality information. The reason for that was most likely due to outdated border station information systems, as well as Foxx's inability to inspire his administrative staff to always stay late at work, to always work hard, and to always strive for perfect accuracy. He then pointed out that if Metexaco's poorly run economy had been put into the capable hands of someone like himself, King Donald, a legendary business professional, instead of a greasy, disgusting, know-nothing hairball like Foxx, then it would have been possible for Metexaco to have made all the long- overdue and much-needed social and technological improvements throughout their kingdom, including modernizing the border station information systems. Unfortunately, King Donald pointed out, Metexaco had Foxx. King Donald sighed at that point in the video, and then wished the people of Metexaco luck.

He waited a few moments to let that sink in, and then, in a much calmer and far gentler manner than I personally would have been capable of, he educated the foreign king on the difference between being the king of the Northern Noble Lands and being the king of a backwater drainage ditch better known as Metexaco. King Donald pointed out, rightfully so, that by being the king of a modern kingdom with a supermassive economy and a cutting-edge military force, he was well within his rights and privileges to do whatever he felt was necessary to ensure the safety and purity of his kingdom. If at times he was to feel a need to exercise his privilege, perhaps by putting certain people in jail whom he considered a cultural threat, like a "brownie" foreigner, then there would be absolutely nothing anyone anywhere would ever be able to do about it. Period.

Then he ended with this: "Perhaps you, King Foxx, would like to jump the border fence sometime and try to tell me how to run my kingdom. I think I would like that a lot. There is nothing I would like better than to have your disgusting greasy brown face beaten to a pulp in front of me by one of my many many loyal and highly trained soldiers while I enjoy my lunch in the palace courtyard."

It was a poignant and beautiful short speech, and I'm sure all citizens of our great kingdom felt the same pride that I did. I nearly cried.

Day Eighty-Five

Over the past couple of days, there have been a few small groups of protesters out in the streets near the capital square. Some seem to think the protests began in response to King Donald's broadcast message to King Suavince of Metexaco, and I'll admit perhaps they did. Personally, I think that anyone who carries around an idiot picket sign to try to make changes to society is obviously unbalanced and should be ignored, or maybe even locked up for observation, and yet, they did actually succeed in getting a generous response from King Donald.

To calm those unhinged idiot Dreamocrat tree-hugging street punk crazy picketers, King Donald reached out to them by announcing a new and exciting two-part social improvement program that night on Fix News. He named the program "Khrump-Fair Charity." During the announcement, he explained to the viewers that he understood and even sympathized with the protesters. He explained that to show his personal commitment to social change, he had come up with a two-part program that he himself had tailored to ensure it addressed their concerns. Part one had to do with clean energy and our environment and our relationship with our neighboring kingdom, Metexaco. A solar panel would be installed on the top of every border fence post that ran along the entire length of our border with Metexaco. Metexaco would be allowed to use the electricity produced by the panels at a reduced rate in order to help provide energy for their border stations. Campground residents with electrician skills would be allowed to assist in the installation of the solar panels, and, to show our kingdom's commitment to the camper's respect and dignity, those who assisted in the installation would receive campground credits which they could spend freely in the campground stores.

Part two of his program showcased King Donald's commitment to the progress of ethnic cultural acceptance in our kingdom. He announced a new and exciting camper sponsorship program that would begin that very evening. For every protest placard that a citizen protester brought in to an official exchange center, the citizen would receive an official cultural acceptance tote bag containing a pair of recycled coconut husk beach sandals, a limited-edition beach towel made from recycled plastic bags, and a voucher good for the release of one complete camp family, with the condition that the citizen agrees to completely provide for all needs of the family. Also included in the bag would be a special railway travel pass good for a one-way trip to the campgrounds, and another set of passes the sponsor could exchange at the campgrounds for passes that would be good for their return trip with their sponsored family. For the sponsor's convenience, the bag would also contain a voucher good for a one- night stay at the processing center just north of the campgrounds.

It was a completely brilliant move by King Donald! Understanding how excitable the protester do-gooder types are, I went down to the exchange centers, and I was really impressed with the turnout. A little later in the evening, as I watched train after train with former protesters leaving the terminal, I kept thinking to myself, "What a wonderful solution! That problem won't be returning again anytime soon."

Day Eighty-Eight

A few peaceful and uneventful days passed by, and then, early on the eighty-eighth day, the Dreamocratic National

Committee just had to start their craziness again. The DNC held a short meaningless press release event at their headquarters, during which they announced they would be asking Cal Jhimly, the Director of Kingdom Security Services, to investigate a series of rumors that had been brought to their attention. They claimed the rumors had to do with criminal actions that had perhaps involved both King Donald and some members of his administration. The timing of the announcement seemed a little strange to me, seeing how King Donald's one-hundredth-day celebration was less than a few weeks away. They were taking a big risk with our good king's patience, and I didn't expect it to end well for the DNC leadership or their organizers.

Interestingly, the DNC headquarters building where they held the event is much different from the modern Repugnican headquarters building. The DNC building has dramatic ancient Greek architectural elements, along with long flowing ribbons of fabric hung from the ceiling, embroidered with all sorts of supposedly inspiring quotes from supposedly important historical figures from our kingdom's past. Seriously, I think the only thing missing from that place is a massive ten-story-tall painted rainbow unicorn which they could plant right outside the front doors. The whole atmosphere of the place sort of explains why their members have such unusual overactive imaginations as well as "holier-than-thou" attitudes. In my humble opinion, their precious "hallowed halls" would be better used if they rented the place out to crazies for comic book conventions or ancient alien theorists conferences.

Anyway, the talking DNC heads listed each accusation, one by one, and, of course, they were all such obvious lies. In total, there were nine accusations, every one of them ridiculous. They ranged from obvious misunderstandings all the way up to the truly bizarre that only an unbalanced mind could possibly believe. I'll list just a few of them here. One standout was the claim that Rodina Hilton was dead. They most likely made this claim because she had not been seen since King Donald's coronation day ceremony. Ridiculous. I guess the DNC representatives never heard of having some time off after a lengthy and particularly draining campaign. Add that to the fact that she lost really badly, and there you go! Who in their right mind would feel like hanging around political reporters after something like that?

Another standout accusation was that King Donald may have "had it in for" and was somehow responsible for the nearly fatal allergic reaction suffered by his favorite office helper and food taster Kandy Anne Conroy. Really? For them to blame King Donald for such a near tragedy was just plain bizarre. What reason could such an upstanding and superbly moral leader such as King Donald possibly have had? If he had gotten tired of looking at her, he could have just fired her. Personally, I would have done just that. While Kandy did have one heck of a figure and face when she first started working for him during the election, she had unfortunately been going downhill and steadily gaining weight since then. We all know that powerful driven men are entitled to see attractive sexually appealing women at work, and there's certainly nothing wrong with that; and yet, because of King Donald's big heart, he kept Kandy on his staff anyway.

One last standout accusation was the claim that King Donald was personally enriching himself at the expense of the individuals living at the campgrounds. They claimed there was a mysterious secret bank account somewhere. No proof, of course, yet they seemed to be absolutely convinced that it was true. Again, the DNC leaders showed themselves to be nothing short of crazy.

A few hours later in the day, Cal Jhimly, the Director of Kingdom Security Services, issued a formal response during a live two-minute press conference he held in the main plaza at the central palace. Cal was obviously embarrassed, and he even publicly apologized for the need to hold such an investigation, and yet, he explained, he must because of the absolute need to keep the public trust. Director Jhimly, a completely loyal subject as well as a personal friend of King Donald and myself as well, assured the kingdom's populace that his investigation would be short, effective, and would reach a conclusion within only a few days. He also promised that it would in no way spoil the upcoming one- hundredth-day celebration.

Day Ninety-One

Unexpectedly, almost like a cheap dime store pulp fiction novel character, Cal Jhimly--yes, THAT Cal Jhimly, the director of the KSS--seemed to have suddenly and inexplicably lost his mind. Completely. In a live early-afternoon televised interview, on the AVN Networks news show VNewsbreak, Cal Jhimly claimed that the rumors the DNC had asked him to investigate a few days prior may actually have had some degree of substance to them after all. As he went over some of the details of the claims, I realized he was either an insane lunatic or a cowardly grotesque disloyal enemy to all the kingdom's citizens--or perhaps, even worse, he was both. In just ten short minutes, he shamed himself and anyone he had ever been associated with. As I watched the interview unfold, I felt stunned, and asked myself what could possibly have gone wrong. After all, Jhimly had been a good friend and a loyal member of our kingdom's court for many many years.

Suddenly, in a flash, I remembered something that had occurred just a few months back. Following his memorable coronation ceremony, King Donald had held a private event for his upper-level administrative workers, the senior officials of the justice department, as well as some trusted senior members of the media. Most of the head staff of Fix News was there, myself included. After a few words from invited speakers and a short break for a light snack buffet, everyone retired to a smaller side room for King Donald's loyalty circle pledging ceremony.

King Donald sat proudly in his twenty-four-karat solid-gold jewel-embellished throne centered in the middle of the room while we, the attendees, stood in a circle around him. One by one, each of us walked up to the king, kneeled before him, bowed our head, pledged our loyalty, and expressed our thanks for the privilege of being allowed to be included in his great plan for the kingdom. We each then kissed his outstretched hand and sucked for a moment on his middle finger. Afterward, we crawled back on our stomachs to our spot in the circle and lay there silently in a fetal position. It was an intense spiritual experience for each and every one of us there, except, I now recalled, for one attendee, Cal Jhimly.

I suddenly remembered that Jhimly, who had been standing to my right during the ceremony, had excused himself to use the restroom, and, I thought to myself, "Wait. He never came back." As I continued watching his interview unfold on the screen, I felt a twinge of guilt because I knew that I should have said something about it that day. Unfortunately, with all the tears and the back-slapping and the bottles of dry but still lightly sweet champagne, I had been too caught up in the moment and I, along with everyone else there, had forgotten all about it. It was an absolute travesty because King Donald and myself, along with everyone else in his administration, should have known better than to have trusted him.

Fortunately, our great King Donald, who at times seems to have more wisdom than even the great "Man Upstairs," issued a televised statement later in the evening to respond to the obviously ridiculous accusations. Afterwards, he kindly invited Director Jhimly, along with any other interested kingdom citizens, to join him at the main palace courtyard event which he would be hosting in two days for a public discussion of the director's findings. The goal, he explained, was to help clear up any possible misunderstandings that might still exist. It was just one more shining example of King Donald's amazing grace and dignified understanding.

Day Ninety-Three

At least fifteen hundred citizens showed up at the plaza for King Donald's public discussion with Director Jhimly. Each individual had been carefully screened to ensure that only the best and most well-informed citizens were allowed in. The event was jam-packed and more than filled to capacity. I was sitting taking notes in an elevated booth that had been provided for the Fix News journalists and camera crew.

A newly constructed stage, painted a deep royal red, had been placed in the center of the plaza. The sun had begun to set and the stage lights that circled the plaza had just come on when both King Donald and Director Jhimly walked out through the palace doors at the edge of the plaza. They paused for a moment to acknowledge the roar of the crowd, and then made their way to the stage, where they sat down. King Donald sat down on a very basic and simple gleaming twenty-four-karat solid-gold throne with glittering gems set into all four posts, while Jhimly made himself comfortable on a beautiful open-back bar-style stool that had been graciously provided for him. Each man had a pedestal microphone set up directly in front of him.

After a few minutes, the crowd began to quiet down. King Donald, who always loves an energetic crowd, took the opportunity to energize it again. He leaned forward and teasingly called out to the crowd, "Hey, are you even out there? I'm waiting." At that moment, instead of the expected "We're here!" response from the crowd, something completely unexpected happened! The crowd went completely silent in an instant. Then, after just a few short moments and some light shuffling sounds, a deafeningly loud screaming erupted from the crowd!

Suddenly, there was an enormous mass of King Donalds, complete with sharp, angry teeth, rushing toward the stage and then flooding onto it like an angry wave from all sides. Somehow, some way, every person in the crowd had on an amazing lifelike mask of King Donald, complete with his beautiful golden hair and his perfect gleaming white teeth, including his very long and dangerously sharp canines. The situation could have been a disaster in lesser hands, but fortunately for Director Jhimly, King Donald was there and would keep him safe. As the fake Donalds tried to drag Jhimly away, King Donald climbed up high on his chair and dove bravely into the swarm. He made his way to Director Jhimly, climbed right up on top of him, and protected him from the crowd. A few moments later, using his amazing strength and agility, he dragged the barely conscious and badly beaten Jhimly through the crowd, off the stage, and up the stairs to the doors of the palace. The two doors opened and closed in a flash with the two of them safely inside.

Incredibly, the mass of Donalds refused to let up, howling insanely and becoming louder and louder as they battered the palace doors, trying to get in. At that point, the guards on the plaza had finally gotten into a defensive position, completely circling the crowd. Suddenly the palace doors flew open and another group of guards came rushing out, down the stairs, and out onto the plaza. King Donald came out a moment later right behind them. As the guards began to subdue the rioters with bean bag projectors and tasers, King Donald walked slowly and calmly to his overturned throne. He grabbed hold of it, stood it back up, and sat down as the guards went through the crowd slapping on handcuffs and tying on gags and muzzles. Luckily, thanks to King Donald's planning for our kingdom's security needs, the guards had been properly equipped to handle all emergency situations, even an unexpected crowd of rioters like the ones there that day. The whole event was quite a sight to see, and the Fix News cameramen made sure they caught all the action.

A short while later, King Donald waved us over and insisted on giving a short interview right there on the plaza even while the protestors were being gathered into groups and taken away for questioning.

"What you've seen here tonight was an absolute tragedy," he began. "The great KSS Director Jhimly, a good and loyal friend to me and many of my closest advisors, was horribly attacked. My promise tonight to everyone in our kingdom is that the individuals responsible for this tragedy will be punished. I have arranged for the entire group to be taken away and questioned at a special security compound. If we ever find out who the ringmaster is, that individual will be punished severely. Unfortunately, as we all know, these types of fanatics almost never give up information about who their leader is. Even knowing that, however, we will still try. We always have hope. What a terrible terrible tragedy. Amazingly terrible, and yet, I can't help but have a great deal of respect for whoever the leader is to have come up with so brilliant a plan. Such an amazing plan. Absolutely amazing. Terrible too of course, but absolutely amazing as well."

"That said, for the time being, for security reasons, I will not be allowing any interviews whatsoever with any of the individuals involved. We all know that every one of them would try to use the opportunity to energize their twisted cause, and I simply cannot allow such a thing. Rest assured, my loyal kingdom citizens, we will get to the bottom of this. As for Director Jhimly, I hope my quick action out there on the plaza will result in our good director's speedy recovery. I ask the great 'Man Upstairs' to help him in his recovery. I will be providing Director Jhimly with everything he could possibly need to recover fully, including of course having his family close at hand. I will personally see to it that they will be kept nearby at all times during his recovery."

"Also, in order to ensure his and his family's complete safety, all will be kept in a secret location known only to myself and a few select individuals during the entire period of his convalescence. Thank you."

Day Ninety-Six

Early in the afternoon, King Donald gave a fascinating live announcement on Fix News- Afternoon Edition that was broadcast direct from the palace rooftop pool patio. Being a less formal event, he decided to forgo the typical stiff-fitting attire and instead wore his favorite generously cut white leisure robe embroidered with his royal crest. His announcement began with him smiling and leaning toward the camera while he sat in his favorite and stunningly beautiful endangered Sumatran rhinoceros leather overstuffed chair.

"Good afternoon, my fellow kingdom citizens," he began. "I've been enjoying a few of my famous Khrump Khornfed Angus steaks this afternoon. Wow, what a treat! Look at this plate, not even the tiniest bit left!"

He held the plate up to the camera to emphasize his point, and yes, those delicious steaks were nowhere to be found. "Everyone in the kingdom should sign up for my Khrump Khornfed Angus steaks of the month club. Take it from me, the ultimate business professional, it's a rock-solid investment in deliciousness! Yes, my friends, being the king does have its perks, and it's good to be the king."

Then, he looked deep into the camera and this time he spoke in a much more serious tone, "My precious kingdom citizens," he began. "The reason for my announcement today is twofold. First, I want to congratulate myself on what I've accomplished so far. Sure, there might have been some little people who helped out along the way with a few small projects, but we all know it's the guy at the top who makes things happen. Over these past nearly one hundred days, I've accomplished so much, and at the same time I've had the most amazing experience of my life being your king. I'm sure it has been an overwhelmingly wonderful experience for all of you as well."

"Yes, I have accomplished so much, and I'm sure you are all very proud. You know, I believe that no king who has ever lived, in this kingdom or any other, has ever accomplished as much as I have in such a short period of time. I truly and absolutely believe that, and hey, keep in mind, the best is yet to come. I'll be making some very special announcements in just a few days on the evening of my One-Hundredth-Day Festival Ball Celebration immediately following the fireworks display. I've put a lot of planning into that celebration, and I'm confident it will be a night to remember. That brings me to the second thing I want to talk about."

He reached over, took a small drink of water, and then leaned very close to the camera looking very serious. "Folks, I have been thinking very long and very hard about what happened to poor Director Jhimly just a few days ago. I've been asking myself, 'What went wrong? Why is no one safe anymore? How could such a terrible thing happen? Did I do something wrong?' Then, in an instant, it came to me. It was as if 'The Man Upstairs' sent me the answer. In that moment I knew. It wasn't me. Of course not. It was you! All of you! Mr. and Mrs. Kingdom Citizen. I ask you now, 'What have you done? How could you do this to the kingdom?'

"How often do any of you think about the responsibility that your freedoms depend on? Probably not very often. Because of this, you have let your freedoms get away from you. You've allowed them to run wild without supervision and, because of your thoughtless and reckless behavior, they have damaged this precious kingdom. They have smashed through your fences, ripped up your lawns, and even torn down your precious homes! You've allowed your long-outdated rights and freedoms to carry out a hideous evil plan against one of the most trusted and respected security organizations, the beloved KSS. This must stop, and it must stop now! It is time for tough love, and I'm going to give it to you!

You have no idea just how lucky you are that I'm here. I have plans and ideas! Huge plans! Huge ideas! You are so lucky I am your king, because I can fix this."

"I had planned to announce the start of Phase One of my five phase Freedoms Directive after the One-Hundredth-Day Festival Celebration, but after what happened to Director Jhimly the other day, I know now that I can't wait. What is it? Well, it's the future. Your future. Listen up, people. Listen up well. It's important. It's all about responsibility, folks. It's about doing what's right for everyone in our sacred kingdom. Yes, responsibility is a mighty big word, but I believe every citizen in our kingdom is big enough to handle it. I am confident of that. We need to be sure your freedoms are tough and strong and effective while at the same time updated and fully modernized. I am sure it is crystal clear to every citizen in our kingdom that safety must be our priority. We must reduce our enemies' ability to carry out attacks, especially in public places."

"Phase One of my directive is all about a modern sense of citizen sacrifice and responsibility. Don't you love the word 'phase'? It's such a futuristic-sounding word. I love it. I'm going to tell you a little story about my own personal sense of sacrifice and responsibility. A few years ago, my wife Ninatina and I were considering adopting a young boy. I was feeling such an overwhelming need to be a parent and to share with a child my life experiences and learned wisdom. Ninatina had an idea that we should find a deserving orphan, perhaps one who had suffered a sickness and was in the process of becoming well. After long weeks of searching the hospital sick wards, we met a very impressive good-looking young orphan boy who had been fighting a rare blood disease for nearly a year. It appeared he had won his battle and the disease was finally in full remission. He certainly seemed to be on his road to recovery.

"Ninatina and I spent some very long and boring weeks going back and forth to the hospital all the while getting to know this little boy better. Both he and the orphanage knew very little of his past. What was known was that he had been dropped into a dumpster when he was only a few days old, and yet fortunately, with some amazing stroke of luck, he was found soon after by a passing jogger who was alerted by the sound of a crying baby. Were his troubles over? No. Sadly, he was a sickly child, and had to spend much of his first few years being shuttled back and forth between the orphanage and various hospitals. I'll tell you this, over those weeks of getting to know him, we could see he was an excitable young boy who wanted nothing more than to have a pair of loving parents and a home to call his own."

"Eventually, the day came when the doctors decided that he was stable and doing well enough to be released back to the orphanage. Ninatina and myself were there that day, and this young boy had put together a small show of sorts in which he sang a few songs he had made up for us. In one of them, he told us both how much he liked us, and in another he told me how someday he wished he would be able to have his name changed to Donald Jr., because he liked and admired me so much. When I heard him say that, I'll admit it gave me a warm fuzzy sort of feeling inside. I've heard they call it a 'father feeling' and, while I'm sure many of the men of the kingdom are familiar with this feeling, it was certainly new to me."

"Well, after what seemed like forever, he was finally done with his little show thing. I stood up, walked over to him, and, not being one to waste time, I looked right in those little blue eyes of his that were brimming with hope and affection and told him, 'No way, kid!' Then, I slapped his face real hard to be sure he got the point."

"You see, as much as I would have enjoyed having a son, I had to put the responsibility that I have to my class first. This is what I mean about sacrifice and responsibility. I understood how it would have been truly irresponsible for me to have taken such an obviously low-quality child into my social group. He was probably from either one of the poor, ignorant lesser-class 'user' families, perhaps even one of the creepy pathetic minorities, or from a classy wealthy deserving family who justifiably threw him away because they could see he wasn't up to their completely reasonable higher standards. Can you imagine how embarrassing it would have been to my important upper-class friends and associates if I suddenly had a son, a Donald Jr., who was such a low-grade inferior quality piece of garbage like him? There was no possible way I could have allowed such a thing to happen. With that in mind, I willingly sacrificed my own wants and needs and took the responsible action that was necessary."

"You know, it's not often that I open up to the public about my personal experiences and feelings, but on this occasion I felt it was necessary for me to do so in order to illustrate my point. Responsibility. It's not easy, but yes, it is necessary. Hey, on a lighter note, it's too bad Ninatina didn't want to adopt a little girl, right? At least in that case, if it hadn't worked out, I'm sure I could have found some reason to keep her around the palace."

"Let's get back to the heavy lifting. Phase One of my Freedoms Directive will begin immediately. I call it 'Freedom Meeting.' Sounds pretty good, right? It is. To ensure our citizens complete safety, for a very short and very temporary ninety days, all public and private meetings will now be prohibited, with one exception only. Our kingdom's finest and most upstanding pre-approved responsible citizens of means will be allowed, if they desire, to submit a petition for a permit for a public or private gathering. The best part? The permit is free! Absolutely no charge at all! Free means free, right? These hand-picked and deserving kingdom citizens will be those who have proven themselves over generations to have true family economic value. This important change to the outdated and old-fashioned traditional 'right to gather' privilege, will ensure that the permit-holder group will have only the best interests in mind for our kingdom. This will give leadership control to only our most productive, freedom-loving citizens. Now, these leadership roles are open to everyone, by the way. It's not important if you belong to one political party or another. Dreamocrat? Repugnican? Who cares? What matters is that our kingdom has the support and guidance of the economically strong: the individuals and families who have proven through time that they deserve to lead. In a way, our system of representation has worked in this way for so long anyway, so I'm just sort of making it official today. Just to be sure that it's clear, the only 'political party' that I care about is the kind I have at the palace every week with my special friends!"

"Oh yes, and before I forget, I promise all of you that even though every member of my office staff is completely overwhelmed by our investigation into the attack on Director Jhimly, we will still be issuing a very complete report on the misunderstandings surrounding his investigative findings. I promise it will be coming very very soon. Our priority right now however, must be your safety. After all, your safety and your sacred freedoms are being threatened."

It was absolutely amazing how King Donald opened up the details of his personal life to his public. I was moved and nearly brought to tears by his frankness and honesty. I think it was one of the best speeches he had ever given. Phase One of his exciting Freedoms Directive was set to begin, and, if you were like me, you felt like you just couldn't wait! I knew the days to come would certainly be memorable as the details of Phases Two, Three, Four, and Five were released! It felt almost as if it was my birthday, and each present was better than the last! I wanted to yell out "More, more, more, and keep them coming!"

Day Ninety-Nine

Day ninety-nine! Just one more to go! It's been a long road, but we're almost there! Already so much has been accomplished, and still so much more coming! I'm so excited because it feels as if the civil rights moment for my class is finally here! Following his announcement of the start of Phase One of his Freedoms Directive, the streets in the capital have been wonderfully calm and beautifully quiet every day and night. I'll admit I did somewhat expect to see small groups of troublemakers holding illegal gatherings as a protest to his directive, but luckily for everyone, it appears as if those poor lost souls have finally done a little growing up and have accepted our kingdom's new reality, our new fair and balanced reality. Of course, it hasn't all been smooth sailing. The Dreamocrats seem to have always had it in for any and all of King Donald's bold yet necessary changes to our kingdom. However, because of our king's persistence and strength of will, as well as, I humbly add, my network's generous assistance, it's all coming together now in an amazing and beautiful King Donald kind of way.

As each day has passed, I've seen how King Donald's policy changes have allowed my class, perhaps the most looked-down-upon class in the history of our kingdom, to receive the recognition that's been so long overdue. We, the upper five percent, are the most valuable yet traditionally underappreciated citizens in our kingdom. Now, at long last, we are coming out of the shadows and finally getting our time in the sun. We are now the freedom leaders.

Today my sources filled me in on when we can expect the start of Phase Two of his Freedoms Directive, shrewdly named Phase Two, Freedom Speech. King Donald will make a formal announcement with full details tomorrow night, with enforcement to begin the following day. The permit procedure will be the same as for Phase One. I sure wish I could be a fly on the wall in the permit application office when the AVN News Network directors try to submit their petition for their Freedom Speech permit! It's about time, right? Their twisted brand of speech will certainly not be missed! I was told Phases Three, Four, and Five will most likely begin just a few days later.

Yes, with the proper leadership in place for all our basic freedoms, by the most responsible and economically respectable citizens, it's easy to see that our kingdom's future will be a much more exciting and dynamic place. These are truly exciting times! I believe that when historians look back, they will see his multi-phase Freedoms Directive as the one that defined his leadership.

Like all strong citizens, I'm ready and willing to make sacrifices and to accept my place in the grand scheme King Donald has planned. I say that because earlier today I received a call from King Donald's wife Ninatina inviting me to sit at the head table with her and our king, along with the kingdom's biggest VIP's. I wasn't surprised that she was the one to call, because I've always considered us special friends. During the few times when we've had the chance to talk over the last few months, we've had such great chemistry. I've told her many times that if she ever found herself lonely and needing someone to talk to, she could count on me to be there for her and to give her unconditional emotional support. Seriously, I think of us as family, and as we all know, having family in high places certainly doesn't hurt. As a matter of fact, when my source in the palace office found out I'd be sitting right next to Ninatina, he leaked to me some details about the event. From what I was told, it's going to be quite an evening! Of course, any event that has King Donald involved is guaranteed to be an over-the-top magnificent spectacle, and judging from what I was told, it will be exactly that: an absolutely fascinating evening of magical enchantment! Here are some details!

Picture walking through the enormous double entryway doors into the Fix News Campus Ballroom and being met with a giant towering circus tent! The entrance into the tent is flanked on both sides by matching solid gold miniature scale-model palaces twenty-five feet tall, each one an exact replica of the main kingdom palace. Entering the tent, you see a long, curving procession of twenty-foot-tall chocolate fountains circling their way around the middle inside of the tent. Behind the ring of fountains is a curving stretch of heavy whitewashed oak tables strung together like an oversized pearl necklace that goes all the way around the inside of the tent. The ring of tables is lined with overstuffed memory foam sofa chairs, each upholstered with the fur or leather hide of the rarest and most beautiful animals in the world--hundreds of species. Behind the seating, the entire length of the canvas tent walls have been beautifully painted with giant angry red elephants battling enormous rainbow-striped crying jackasses--a passionately created work of art done in a classic Warhol meets Picasso meets DaVinci style. The epic story of our kingdom's struggles!

With the guests seated facing the center rings, they'll each enjoy an amazing and sumptuous meal served to them on a polished twenty-four-karat solid-gold plate, all the while enjoying their favorite beverage from a gleaming twenty-four-karat solid-gold goblet.

Even the servers will be top-shelf! King Donald wants only the most beautiful ten-to-twelve-year-old young girls bussed in from the "brownie" and "scarfhead" vacation campgrounds to service the event. While the guests enjoy the magical lush sounds of a blaring circus pipe organ, a series of live animal acts will begin, followed by a high wire acrobatics show featuring the famous daredevil clown Scaramucci, who always performs without a net. Of course, there are some people who are put off by the famous clown's reliably crude and sometimes grotesque physical comedy, and yet, seeing how all the guests there will be adults, and the fact that King Donald happens to completely adore him, it was decided he'd fit in very well with the evenings theme. I hesitate to write this next part because it just seems too great to be true, and I'm hoping my source wasn't just pulling my leg.

The most incredible surprise of all is that instead of sitting at the head table watching the show unfold, King Donald himself will be the circus ringmaster! Imagine that!

The amazing circus acts will only be possible because, while King Donald's longtime friend King Putenski of Pruska did send his regrets for not being able to come for the celebration, he did send his entire family circus to serve as the evening's entertainment! Of course, just in case some guests prefer a more gently paced evening, the side offices of Fix News will be screening small arthouse-style films, mostly early twentieth century black and white eight-millimeter silent pornography. For those guests who enjoy the retro club scene, other offices will be transformed into late-midcentury discotheques, complete with mirrored dance floors and young beautiful girls in cages. I was told that King Donald was so enthusiastic about the evening events that he told the planners, "If, by some strange stretch of the imagination, someone doesn't like the circus acts or the arthouse porn, it's a sure bet they'll love the discos with the beautiful girls in cages. After all, anyone who doesn't like beautiful girls in cages has got to have a screw loose!"

Honestly, when I heard about that mighty quote from our king, I thought to myself, "THAT is why I love King Donald!"

The biggest night of the year, the biggest party of the year, and the most important people of the year, and I'll be there! Me, your humble newsman, is even sitting at the head table as one of the VIP's! Well, it sure does seem as if everything is coming up roses for everyone these days!

One hundred days! The benchmark for the future! Can you believe it?

Day One Hundred
EDITOR'S NOTE

The entry for day one hundred was never written. Phil O. Reilly, along with his colleagues Hannah Seanity and Lewis

Dobson, were killed during the explosions that occurred during the One-Hundredth-Day Festival Ball held at the Fix News Complex. That same evening, King Donald and his wife Ninatina disappeared and are presumably being held for ransom, although strangely enough, as of the time I write this, there has still been no ransom demand received from anyone, according to what I've been told by the department of Kingdom Security Services.

My name is Anson Kuper, and I'm the chief editor at Kingdom Books. Kingdom Books is a small publishing company which, in the past, has very rarely done business with high-profile celebrity writers such as Mr. Reilly. My company was contacted by Mr. Reilly's representatives after his usual preferred publishers passed on this, his final and not quite complete book. Of course, it's just pure speculation on my part, but I suspect the reason his usual publishers decided to pass on this, his final work, may have had something to do with the unusual circumstances surrounding how Mr. Reilly and his colleagues' bodies were found during the excavation. That same reason may also explain why not only his publishers, but also his business associates, as well as his usually loyal and adoring rabid Repugnican fan base seem to want to have nothing more to do with him or his memory. I will elaborate on this a little later.

In keeping with the spirit of Mr. Reilly's intentions for this book, I will be filling in the details about what happened on the evening of the One-Hundredth-Day Celebration, beginning just prior to the attack. In addition, I will be providing the few bits of information that have been uncovered so far by the KSS during their investigation into who may be responsible.

Phil O. Reilly

The Evening of the One-Hundredth-Day Celebration

According to the hundreds of "top five percenters" who were there that night, and who enthusiastically agreed to be interviewed for this book, Fix News was host to the most grotesque evening of hedonistic depravity our kingdom has ever seen. That, by the way, is not just my somewhat prudish assessment of the evening, but is instead the actual proudly enthusiastic opinion of every one of the individuals I interviewed. Suffice it to say it was an evening of pure "King Donald debauchery."

The celebration had been in full swing for a few hours when Ninatina informed her personal guard she wanted to go back to the palace for a short rest because the extreme level of noise from the celebration had given her a severe headache. Just a few minutes afterward, King Donald headed back to the palace as well to change from his red ringmaster costume with the golden shoulder tassels to a more formal and appropriate black tuxedo, which he planned to be wearing when he addressed the crowd after the fireworks display.

It was at this point that inside the giant tent and above the center ring, all guests' eyes were trained on Mr. Scaramucci, who was about halfway through his act. Ninety feet up and at the midway point of the high wire, Scaramucci was gingerly balancing on the top rung of a ladder back chair, which was itself balancing on the wire with a single back leg. Next came a short drumroll, after which he unzipped his baggy clown pants and let them drop to his knees. A few seconds later the "clown," who King Donald and most of the wealthiest individuals in our kingdom like to refer to as a "comedy genius," began the trademarked high-wire self-pleasuring part of his act.

As the crowd of our kingdom's new "Freedom Leaders" looked on with intense fascination at the depravity taking place overhead, an emergency announcement came in over the Fix News intercom system. Unfortunately, with the intense level of noise coming from the pipe organ, the crowd, and the animal trainers who were shouting at their barely controlled circus animals, there was no way for anyone to hear the announcement. A few minutes later, a large group of Fix News interns came running into the tent yelling that everyone needed to evacuate immediately because a bomb threat had just been called in to the main receptionist station. Of course, this sudden unexpected announcement started a panic and all at once everyone headed for the tent exit.

Unfortunately for Scaramucci, the spotlight operators ran for the exits along with the guests, causing the spotlights to swing quickly down and face the ground, which disoriented Scaramucci, who was still ninety feet above the ground with no net below him. With his clown pants around his ankles, Scaramucci slipped and fell toward the ground and would have been killed if not for the elephant below him. Landing hard on the elephant's back, he rolled off and fell to the ground, at which point a pair of campground server girls grabbed his arms and dragged him out of the building. He was badly hurt but still very lucky to be alive. I'm no doctor, but after a fall like that, I'm pretty sure his career is over. I tried to get the names of the server girls who helped him, but was told that all the server girls had not had identification cards issued to them, and that each had been told that if they happened to be asked what their names were, they were to answer by choosing one of three names: Melody, Candy, or Bambi.

After about five minutes, all guests and workers were safe and out of the building, with the exception being the three Fix News journalists Reilly, Seanitty, and Dobson. No one had been able to find them, so it was assumed they had gone to get help. It was then that a series of explosions ripped through the ballroom wing of the news complex, and, in just a few moments, it was over. The entire ballroom wing had collapsed and fallen into the basement storage area and bathroom lounges below. The enormous crowd looked on in astonishment and disbelief at the burning wreckage and wondered how such a tragedy could have occurred. Three days later, during the excavation of the wreckage, the bodies of the three Fix journalists were found huddled together on a pair of couches that had pushed together in the lower level bathroom lounge. Later, it was found that tragically, for some unknown reason, the intercom system for the lower lounge area of the complex had never been completed, which meant that the warning to exit the building wasn't heard by anyone in that area. It goes without saying that it was a terrible terrible tragedy.

Now I've arrived at what I feel may be the reason for Mr. Reilly's sudden unpopularity among his normally dedicated yet obnoxious and bigoted small-minded supporters. I've personally never had a fondness for salacious news journalism, although the three Fix News journalists who were killed there that evening most certainly did. All three were very well known for their so called "Special Moral Reports" during which, through blatant misrepresentation and outright lies, they promoted fear, mistrust, and condemnation, as well as acts of violence toward anyone in the gay, lesbian, or transsexual community. It is because of their combined history of hate toward others who were different that, in the interest of fairness as well as exposing extreme hypocrisy, I report the following.

During the excavation that was done to find and remove

the journalists' bodies from the wreckage, the three were found in what I've been told is referred to as a "train" position. As if that by itself was not unusual enough, even more unusual is how their "train" was assembled. Their "train hookup" would only be possible if they each had the genitals of the opposite sex which, I was told, and the medical examiner confirmed, was indeed the case. Yes, you read that right. The Fix News journalists who promoted all forms of hate and discrimination against those who were different were themselves quite different.

The Week Following the Attack

In the days that followed, a terrible chaos washed over the kingdom. Rioting was widespread, and with it came massive property destruction. King Donald's supporters and detractors screamed and fought all day, every day, each side seeming to want to destroy the other, which in turn brought a deeper and more terrible despair to everyone. As if that wasn't enough, there was a feeling of complete dread about what might possibly be coming next.

Surprisingly, no one came forward to claim responsibility for the attack. According to the KSS expert analysis, such a daring combination attack and kidnapping could only have been carried out by an experienced professional group of terrorists. After the first week of intense investigation, only two facts seemed solid: the person who called in the bomb threat was most likely a woman, and the analysis of the explosive residue showed it contained crude ingredients that were easily accessible everywhere throughout the kingdom. Their investigation will of course continue.

Oddly, there was no police or military response to the rioting at all, anywhere, not even in the streets and parks that surround the palace. There was not one single attempt made by the police or any branch of the military to try to interfere in any violent outbreaks. There was also no attempt by any government office to enforce any of the five phases of King Donald's Freedom Directive. It was almost as if, without King Donald to guide them, all levels of government, including both civil and military police forces, were lost and unsure of what actions to take, and so did nothing.

After the kidnapping, for reasons that are unclear, King Donald's weekly popularity and approval polling continued. According to the polls, up until a few days before his disappearance, his average approval rating had been holding steady around thirty percent. Following his disappearance however, his support slid backwards to the low twenties. Why? Well, it's possible it could have been related to the announcement of his multiphase Freedoms Directive, however, without more specific polling, there's no way to tell if that was the case. Of course, while King Donald's support among the citizenry had lessened, that is not to say his supporters were not a force to be reckoned with, because they were. Perhaps they always will be.

Where We Are Now

As this book goes to press, the general mood in the kingdom remains grim. There have, however, been some uplifting developments. The most important of these is that we appear to have proof that King Donald is alive. Just a few weeks ago, a little over a month after he and his wifes disappearance, a medium-sized wooden crate overflowing with notebooks and file folders was left on the back loading platform near the rear exit door here at Kingdom Books. The editorial staff was having a meeting that morning, and we were in the middle of discussing this very same book when two loading-dock workers strolled into our conference room with the crate on a dolly, and asked, "Was this supposed to be outside?"

For a few moments, we all just stared at the crate. The single word "IMPORTANT" was written boldly in metallic gold paint on one of its sides, and, as if that wasn't unusual enough, that was a bright red "sealed with a kiss" puckered lips impression over the letters "NT." We all sort of scratched our heads for a few seconds to take it all in, and then had them place the crate on the conference table. After a few minutes of discussion along with some poking at its contents, we had a plan.

While some of us removed folders and notebooks and quickly read through them while taking notes, others made copies for us to study later in more detail. We felt comfortable making copies, because we were unable to find any "classified" or "secret" or copyright stamps on any of the material. After a short while, the general feeling in the room was that what we had in our possession was most likely tied to the investigation that had been spearheaded by Cal Jhimly, the KSS Director, who, by the way, has not been heard from.

It was obvious the contents of that simple wooden crate had the potential to be devastating for King Donald, if, of course, it could be verified as accurate. It contained not only information related to the accusations that had been made against King Donald by the AVN Network and the DNC, but also additional information concerning previously unknown criminal activities, some of which was absolutely horrifying, that had unintentionally come to light during Jhimly's investigation.

Hours later, when we were finally getting to the files at the bottom of the crate, we found it. Lying flat on the bottom was a single VHS video tape labeled "The King." Someone grabbed it, held it up, and shouted "Do we have a player for this?"

Luckily, we did. There was an old VHS player in the storage basement, so we had it brought upstairs and connected to our conference room monitor. Then, with no one knowing what to expect, we hit "play." The video began with a close-up of a newspaper, with the focus on the publication date. After a few seconds, the newspaper was pulled away, revealing a parade taking place in the distance. After a few seconds more, it became clear that King Donald was the one leading the parade. We viewed the entire tape, about two minutes long, and afterwards for about fifteen seconds, we stood in stunned silence.

Finally, someone blurted out, "Was that real?" to which someone else replied, "Of course it was! That was huuuuge! Amazing! Best, video, ever!" which made everyone laugh nervously, myself included. A moment later someone shouted, "Play it again!" and we did, again and again and again, for about an hour.

Now, while I admit we book editors typically like to think of ourselves as quiet, reserved, and somewhat dignified individuals, we do at times, with the right stimulation, become excitable and rowdy like children at recess, which is pretty much how we were that day after viewing the tape. Why? Well, that tape was really…*special*.

Early the next day, we repacked the crate with all the original notebooks, files, and video tape, then delivered the whole thing over to KSS headquarters. We were pretty sure they'd find it interesting.

Next, we decided the video tape would be best used as a promotional tool to gather publicity for the upcoming release of Mr. Reilly's book. The popular downtown pub Gigglin' Gill's graciously agreed to allow Kingdom Books to host a video premiere of the tape in their central dining area. Gigglin' Gill's was a good choice because of its popularity with the lower and middle classes, plus they had a large enough space for the crowd we were hoping for.

To promote the premiere, we contacted the AVN Network and made a deal. They agreed to provide television advertising on their network for both the video premiere and Mr. Reilly's book, as well as a live broadcast from Gill's that night, but only on the condition that we partnered with them for researching and verifying the information that had come from the crate. It made sense, seeing how much quicker the work could be accomplished, so we agreed.

Kingdom Books will at some point publish a King Donald tell-all type book and the AVN Network will have plenty of fuel for their news shows. A win-win for both. You may be asking yourself why we chose the AVN Network instead of the Fix News Network. We chose them because the Fix News Network had already provided such a heroic public service to our kingdom after having been chosen by King Donald to be his and his administration's official news network. We felt Fix News had already done more than enough. The AVN Network seemed to us to be the most "fair and balanced" choice.

Gigglin' Gill's Grogg and Grubb Pub

The AVN Network broadcast live from Gigglin' Gill's on the night of the premiere. They broadcast not only the showing of the tape but also the crowd's reaction. One of the evening's biggest surprises was when, a few minutes before the showing, Rodina Hilton walked in. She walked past the bar and straight through the crowd, not stopping until she got to the few rows of chairs that had been set up near the wide-screen TV. She sat in the chair closest to the TV and didn't move. This was a huge surprise because nearly everyone had assumed, as I did, that she was dead. It wasn't very long until a few people started walking over, I assumed to ask her where she had been.

As they got close to her, she turned, put up her hand and said, at the top of her voice, "If anyone so much as puts a finger on me, I will kick their ass all the way to the Metexaco border!" after which she lowered her hand and turned back to the empty screen. As seven o'clock came nearer, I instructed the crowd to quiet down so I could start the tape, and, at seven o'clock sharp, I pressed "play."

The crowd seemed a little confused when the newspaper was pulled back from the lens, but then cheered when they saw the parade in the distance being led by King Donald. The parade marchers were dressed for very cold weather, with their faces hidden beneath scarves and bulky winter hats. Whoever was filming the parade began walking toward it.

After about ten seconds, Rodina Hilton, alone in the seating area and much closer to the screen than everyone else, saw something. She leaned forward in her seat and stared at the screen for a moment. Suddenly, she jumped up screaming "Lock him up! Lock him up! Lock up that pig and throw away the key!" Lock him up!"

The room was completely silent. A few moments later, everyone realized what she had seen. The person recording the parade had walked from along the side of the parade to the front. From that vantage point, it was easier to see that King Donald was wearing heavy shackles on his hands and feet. There were armed guards behind him and on both sides. The parade continued for a half minute more before arriving at the end of the street, where it stopped.

King Donald stood facing a large heavily constructed cage. Hanging above the door of the cage was a gold plaque with the inscription "My Favorite Possession," which seemed to be the plaque that had been stolen from the Khrump Compound several months ago. A man with an enormous fur hat and thick winter coat was standing next to the cage. He spoke to King Donald, opened the cage door, and pushed him inside. He said something again, then closed and locked the door.

The person filming walked closer to the cage and stopped just off to the side. King Donald turned quickly and snarled at the person holding the video camera, but then quickly changed his expression to one of shock and hurt. This is when he spoke for the first and only time in the video.

He asked, "Why would you do this? How can you do this to me?"

At this point, we learned the person with the camera was a woman. She responded to King Donald, her voice breaking as she spoke, "I'm sorry. This is what you deserve. This is where you belong."

www.ingramcontent.com/pod-product-compliance
Lightning Source LLC
Chambersburg PA
CBHW021913180426
43198CB00034B/366